Endorse

"When women journey into the depths of their heart to bare their soul, the whole world awakens with them. Empowered Voices is a beacon of light, not to be missed!"

~ANDREA COSTANTINE~
Co-Creator of the Speaking Your Truth: Courageous Stories from Inspiring Women
http://andreacostantine.com/

"It can be so easy to get stuck in your story; to allow yourself to be defined by a tragedy or loss. But how do you move forward after hurt and violation? How do you stop making excuses and start making a difference? Empowered Voices is a wake-up call for us all. Each provocative chapter is proof that we have a choice about whether we will be prisoners of our past and circumstances, or conscious creators of our life. Proof that fully living requires fully opening our eyes."

~SUSAN BISHOP, CPCC~
Creativity & Innovation Coach
Unlocked Box, Inc.
http://www.unlockedbox.com

"Here are twenty-three Empowered Voices -- gifting the reader with deeply intimate, articulate reflections on the power of innate wisdom and vibrancy. This book is a beautiful tribute to the process of awakening, lovingly shepherded by Andrea Hylen."

~KAREN RIBEIRO~
Author and Life and Business Coach
http://www.innerfortune.com/

"Collections of short stories are only as powerful as the inspiration behind them and the thread that binds them. "Empowered Voices" harmonically emerge from a deep place, crafted through a partnership these twenty-three women formed and driven by Andrea Hylen's brilliant process of inward journeying through community. Individually and collectively, you will feel the chords these women strike as they reverberate right into your heart. From the striking metaphors each author summons to the agonizing lessons they have transmuted into hope and confidence, these women offer a truly gentle gift of support and inspiration."

~ELLEN KORONET~
Principal at LNK Creative, LLC
Marketing Research for the Entrepreneurial Spirit
www.LNKCreative.com

"One of the most powerful tools people have are the words used to connect to one another. Telling our heartfelt stories in an open and honest way changes our vibration, lifting all who are touched by the passages. Never underestimate the power of women who have found their path. "Empowered Voices: True Stories by Awakened Women" conveys what we all know in our center--that we are unlimited potential. Women are waking up to their vocal chords and this book is what it sounds like when put to paper, reading their stories, you hear your own. It fills me up to be connected to such integrity."

~LAURISSA HELLER~
Author, Radio Show Host, Astrologer
www.blogtalkradio.com/theweeklyvibe

"Reading the stories in this book I recognize how many things that happen to us effect our lives. Often we are who we are because of what happened, but, if we are wise, we become who we are in spite of what happens to us. These courageous women have given us a glimpse into what it's like to rise above circumstance and live out loud."

~REV. GRACE LOVEJOY~
Center for Spiritual Living, Camarillo, CA
http://www.cslcamarillo.org/

"Courageous are these women to speak out. And Archangel Ariel blesses all of these words. These transforming stories help us stand up in the light for our beliefs-- and know that we are spinning gold of what was into greatness."

--LORE RAYMOND~
Founder & Chief Inspirator, Women as Visionaries
www.WomenasVisonarieswithLoreRaymond.com

Andrea Hylen's Empowered Voices gives voice to ALL women, regardless of our personal journeys. It includes beautifully crafted stories ranging from traumatic experiences to the stuff of every day life. Every woman's story spoke to some part of me, and moved me deeply. Empowered Voices is a must read for any woman who is on a journey to know herself better – and to show up as the authentically powerful woman she truly is.

~MARIAN HEAD, Author, Keynote Speaker~
Revolutionary Agreements
http://revolutionarychoices.com/

Empowered Voices

True Stories by Awakened Women

Heal My Voice, Inc
Santa Monica, California

Empowered Voices: True Stories by Awakened Women

Copyright © 2012 Heal My Voice, Inc and Andrea Hylen

Published by:
Heal My Voice, Inc
Andrea Hylen
Santa Monica, CA 90401
www.healmyvoice.org

ISBN 13: 978-0615685694
ISBN-10: 0615685692

Cover design by Josie Thompson Designs, Inc
Editor: Andrea Hylen

Printed in the United States of America

A portion of the proceeds from the sale of this book will be donated to further the work of Heal My Voice.

Dedication

To ALL of the readers:

We see you.

We know who you really are.

Our stories are dedicated to you
and your brilliant essence.

We encourage you to write your story now and to
shine your light in your home, your community
and the world.

We are listening.

Blessing

We bless the ancient yearning that is calling; a voice that is reaching up from the deep sacred, beckoning you to reacquaint yourself with the knowledge that the entirety of your life has been in service to evolution and healing.

May you enter into these pages in the most sacred of ways and know, absent of any doubt, the cathartic potential woven into the intimate sharing of these stories.

May the authors be blessed by an exponential exchange of humble gratitude for the courage and willingness to share such bold stories of transformation.

May you, the recipient of this empowering collection, receive these words as prayers for your own revelation of the inborn power you possess to transcend any and all stories of pain, lack and limitation.

May you discover your wings and fly mightily towards your dreams.

May you reawaken to a destiny that is revealed through the perfection that is unfolding in perpetual motion with your willingness to surrender to a higher perspective in the telling of your own stories.

In reality, it takes one moment to completely alter the trajectory of one's life; one moment of decision to be welcoming to the transformation that is wanting to take place within you, within all women, and therefore, within the whole of humanity.

May you know that you are the ONE…after all…

It Takes Just One

It takes just one…One moment, one breath, one decision.
It takes just one…One person, one action, one prayer.
It takes just one…One smile, one word, one act of faith, one
courageous, willing step towards the bigger yes and the
deeper why, the reasons you exist and were awakened to a
new day where you could say "Yes!" when given the choice
and release all other alternatives.
It takes just one…One step, one hug, one ear to listen, one
choice to forgive.
It takes just one life dedicated to love for the whole world to
change, for a life to be lived from aliveness, for a new creation
to be born, and for healing to occur…
You are the One…the only, the everything within the whole to
make a difference today.
So, take one moment to ask yourself the question…

What do I wish to give life to today?

~Anita Pathik Law

Anita (Ani) Pathik Law, CFCC, CHt, is a coach, hypnotherapist, lyricist, published author, speaker, healing facilitator, and a powerful voice in the consciousness movement. Author of The Power of Our Way; A Path to a Collective Consciousness, founder of The Power of Our Way Community and host of Conscious Dialogues, for over 17 years she has worked with thousands of people around the globe to help them "Raise Consciousness and Take Responsibility for Their Own Shift." Known as a "midwife to the soul," Anita has leveraged the power of the mind and spirit to overcome the seemingly impossible. She guides her clients to tap into their own mastery by awakening to and aligning with their soul's purpose to receive their inknown wisdom and gifts. A modern day shaman and energy alchemist who weaves both her East Indian heritage and indigenous spiritual practice into her work with healing and business clients, she offers a unique and spiritually grounded approach to all that she does and is in the world.

Receive a powerful audio download of "A Declaration to Receive Your Good" at
www.powerofmyway.com/ideclare.html

TABLE OF CONTENTS

Part One: I AM Powerful

Part Four: I AM Beauty

FOREWORD

Ann Quasman

Host of WomanTalkLive

I am truly honored to have been asked to be a part of this important book. Important because it shares the stories of twenty-three women who *woke up* and claimed something of real value that belonged to them; something that was already there, but which had been hidden away, put to the side or just forgotten. In other words, stories of women who woke up and found themselves – who claimed the truth of who they were, and made conscious decisions about what they were willing to let go of and how they would choose to live going forward. Powerful stuff.

According to the dictionary on my computer, the official definition of the word "empower" is to give the authority or power to do something or make someone stronger and more confident, especially in controlling their life and claiming their rights. As for "awaken," the definition is to rouse from sleep, cause to stop sleeping or to make someone aware of something for the first time.

In every sense, these women woke up and became empowered – they aroused themselves from a deep sleep and became conscious creators of their own lives.

When I think about my own waking up and re-discovery, I often wonder what took me so long. I believe that

I came out of the womb and was shortly thereafter programmed to run on autopilot for most of the next forty-three years.

It all began with the performance I call my Trick Dog Phase – a stage of my life during which I tried to gain approval from everyone. Especially my parents.

Good grades and Dean's List were my priorities. So was looking good, getting a great job after college, being promoted and marrying "well." All of these things I thought signified importance and power – and they seemed to please the people I was trying to please most.

Then, I had an epiphany (a.k.a. a vision brought on by total exhaustion and having "no life").

After spending almost twenty years married to my job and the corporate ladder I was climbing – not to mention, living on prescription painkillers to deal with the effects of a college car accident, smoking close to two packs of cigarettes a day, not eating well, drinking too much and clubbing on weekends, plus dealing with a frightening sexual assault that altered my life – I began what was to be a long process of waking up.

At that point, I was very far from knowing my truth. I was no where close to leading the life I wanted to live and, more importantly, I had strayed very far away from my own heart. Clearly, something had to give. I left corporate America, much to the shock of everyone who thought they knew the real me.

Today, I'm forever grateful for what finally got my attention. It wasn't a strike of lightening or a Kundalini experience. It was a book handed to me by a stranger. A book called *The Wisdom of Florence Scovel Shinn*.

Florence was wise indeed. She let me know that my thoughts are powerful and that I can create my life without permission or approval from others – a monumental lesson for approval seeking, people-pleasing me.

Armed with this new knowledge, I embarked on the journey to reclaim myself, thankful for the many teachers, opportunities and communities that facilitated my transformation along the way. When you are ready, they are there waiting for you, too.

During my process, one of my biggest Ah-Ha's was how much I missed having women in my life. Sure, I had girlfriends growing up and in college, but as an adult I worked in the company of men. I was starving for female companionship and I wanted to be in a community of women.

Inspired by this realization, I created a series of workshops specifically for women who, like me, had experienced emotional traumas and wanted to heal. Teaching allowed me to go more deeply into myself, to find those parts of me that had been hidden away. Even more, it allowed me to get to know women, to listen to them, to learn from them, and to be part of their open-armed community.

At that point, an unexpected opportunity presented itself: The opportunity to create and host a live radio show. That show, WomanTalk Live, has allowed me to take my relationships with women to exciting new places. It's allowed me to have deeper conversations about how we as women are living our lives and the issues that affect us, our families, our communities and our world.

Plunked down between male-dominated programming, WomanTalk Live has evolved into a true community of women (and lots of men, too) who actively engage in a more conscious conversation. Facilitating these conscious conversations with listeners, readers, community members, show sponsors and those who are making a difference for women is my passion.

As I become more and more comfortable using my voice, more and more projects seemed to emerge from my passion. I created *Girls Gone Great*, a scholarship essay contest for female high school juniors and seniors. Each year, Girls Gone Great recognizes a young woman who's making a big difference in her community now, and who also has a plan to take her vision forward. What an incredible experience it has been to find so many young women with amazing strength who are already living their lives true to their purpose.

My latest project is called the *Conscious Conversations Café* and I could not be more thrilled about the concept and where it's taking me.

Conscious Conversations Cafés occur about four to six times per year on the WomanTalk Live radio show. I bring three women into the studio to discuss a topic of interest to women: How does a midlife crisis show up for a woman; What it's like to be a mommy entrepreneur running a business and a home; Escaping domestic violence and creating a new life; The power of resilience; Why women will change the world; Coming out as gay at work; and recently, Writing to heal with some of the co-authors of *Fearless Voices: True Stories by Courageous Women,* the very first Heal My Voice book circle project.

These live radio show conversations are unplanned, authentic and come from the heart of each guest. They are among the most listened to shows in WomanTalk Live's podcast archive.

Soon, *Conscious Conversations Café* will evolve into a live lecture series held at Goucher College in Baltimore several times each year. My plan is to bring nationally recognized women thought-leaders together with college students and members of our community for a conscious conversation about a topic critical to women. The proceeds from the live events will benefit a cause that is near and dear to my heart: the Maryland Coalition Against Sexual Assault (MCASA). I also serve on MCASA's board of directors and this appointment, along with the funds the Conscious Conversations Café will raise, mean that I'm now an active advocate and voice for sexual assault survivors. My mantra is "no more silence" and forwarding this message is one of the great works of my life.

When I look back at what has transpired over the past ten to fifteen years, I attribute it all to my original "waking up" and am grateful to have finally heard the alarm.

Each painful incident, each lesson along the way, each success has integrated with my being and become a piece of the foundation that allows me to stand at a higher place with a much broader view.

I often feel like the elephant who after years of being contained by a tiny little rope around her ankle, realizes that it's just a tiny rope. The freedom this awareness brings is amazing and suddenly, in a still evolving way, all the things I know at a soul level bubble to the surface. I can finally claim the real me with an empowered voice and share myself with others. It's a process and I'm still transforming. But my mission is clear: To each day, start a conversation that in some way moves even one woman from talking to doing.

I'm grateful to the community of women who have helped me come this far and to the many more who will cross my path and provide even more encouragement and inspiration in the future – like the twenty-three awakened women who share their stories of finding and using their empowered voices in this book.

Each story provides us with an opportunity to witness a woman stepping forward and sharing her truth from a place of deep knowing. Each woman becomes a role model for other women, demonstrating that when we tune into the essence of who we are, and when we are willing to speak up and out and live that truth, nothing will ever be the same.

This is the real gift of this book.

Ann Quasman *is a woman on a mission. Her goal is to encourage and facilitate conscious conversations that will help women connect with and rely upon the wisdom within their hearts as much as they do the wisdom within their minds. As host of WomanTalk Live and the creator of the Conscious Conversations Café, Ann brings women everywhere deeper into topics that both inspire and inform. Find out more at* ***www.WomanTalkLive.com*** *and* ***www.ConsciousConversationsCafe.com***.

Acknowledgements

To all of the writers and community members connected with this project, thank you for saying, "Yes!" You held the space for something new to emerge from each of us in a secret Facebook group, on group phone calls, in individual coaching sessions and in workshops. It was your courage and willingness to write one vulnerable word at a time that made this book project come to life.

I bow down in gratitude to each of you for trusting me and calling me into greater leadership. You held a safe space with me...for each woman to step into a fuller expression and offer her unique leadership in the group. Believing in each other created an environment for bursts of brilliance. The week we ALL read our stories out loud was one of the most powerful, vulnerable, intimate experiences of my life. Your words...your voices...your unique expression...Better than chocolate and fireworks and a spectacular sunset!

The sacred space of reading led Yana Mileva to suggest an audio book and Charlene Sansone stepped into her brilliance. Holding the space, sharing her technical skills and hours too numerous to count! Our voices out in the world! All thanks to you!

Ellen Koronet, you have become my most trusted editor, word muse, word smith or whatever it is you do to help me see where my words want to travel. Thank you for jumping in to read my story, the introduction, and offer your fresh perspective and creative expression. Thank you for continuing to cheer me on to the finish line!

Thank you to David Morelli, who created an energy coaching program and provided a space for all of us to meet and build a strong community. Connecting with the authors in this book was one of many amazing gifts in the year-long program.

Karen Porter...your belief in this process and all of the

energy you bring to it is an important element in driving this train. Thank you for fully stepping into the role of President of the Board of Directors and for picking me up whenever I think I can't take one more step. You have held the vision with determination, grace and Love. Eternal gratitude!

To my three daughters, Mary, Elizabeth and Hannah who continue to be the carrots at the end of the stick that compel me to grow, stretch and heal my own voice over and over again. You have inspired me to always reach to be the best role model of a woman living life and growing into her fullest potential. Stay tuned! The best is yet to come!

And finally a huge thank you to a woman named Kimnore who is currently residing in a prison in Arkansas. After reading a story called, "Running to Heal," by Karen Ribeiro in the first Heal My Voice book project, "Fearless Voices: True Stories by Courageous Women," she was inspired to write a poem.

I am so grateful she shared it with us...

RUNNING
By Kimnore

I've spent my life running from here to there,
Running from things too painful for me to bear.

I've spent my life running from place to place,
Running from stuff too painful for me to face.

I've spent my life running always trying to hide,
Always running from the pain deep down inside.

I've spent my life running from a lot of stuff,
But I couldn't seem to ever run far enough.

I've finally stopped running long enough to see,
That all along what I'd been running from was me.

~May 2012

———

Introduction

Andrea Hylen

Founder of Heal My Voice

In the Spring of 2012, I was immersed in supporting and creating a safe space for the twenty-three authors of the powerful stories in this second, "Heal My Voice" book publication. One vulnerable word at a time, these successful women were reclaiming hidden aspects of their own personal power: writing to heal a story in their lives.

As I settled into my living room to fold laundry one cozy evening, I came upon a replay of an Alfred Hitchcock movie. All in black and white, the camera slowly zoomed in to focus on a husband cooking breakfast for his wife. They lived in a camping trailer and you could see the wife sleeping in the bed next to the kitchen. As the camera followed the husband carrying a tray of eggs, toast and coffee towards the bed, the wife began to yawn with cooing sounds of love and recognition and a soft "good morning," stretch. He leaned down, carefully balancing the tray and kissing her on the cheek. Nuzzling her with his lips, cheek to cheek, he snuggled up to her ear, whispering softly, "Hey Worthless."

When I heard those two little words, I froze instantly, with an unfolded bath towel in my hands, standing stock still in disbelief.

What? WHA-WHAT? "Hey WORTHLESS?"

Those words had been offered as a term of endearment and a declaration of love. If I wasn't so keenly aware of the power of words, I might have missed those two, slippery units of language wedged between the kisses and breakfast food. It was subtle. "Hey Worthless" was spoken with the energy of love, affection, a smile, a soft touch, a stroke of the hair and was accompanied by a tray full of nourishment.

It may seem like I am making a big deal about such a small phrase but the "Hey Worthless" message exploded in my ears like a trumpet blast. While we could debate the genius of Hitchcock and his cleverly disguised insult, the blasting in my ears created a frozen state in my body. This was one of the ways women had been programmed to think they were worthless, less than, not enough or wrong. This is how their voices were shut down. It began with one slippery, biting word at a time; demeaning, dishonoring, invalidating abuse intermixed with food, shelter, belonging, and "love." From men, from women, from the media and more...

Growing up, we received subtle messages from loved ones and strangers: hey clumsy, she's such a slob; don't beat the boys at that game because they won't like you. You're too much, too loud, too intense... lighten up, have a sense of humor, get over it, don't be so serious, go along with the crowd. And underneath the subtle words that were chipping away at our spirit and confidence, many of us had our innocence violated both physically and emotionally with physical and verbal abuse. We were told that we had caused it and deserved it!

It is no wonder that our voices were shut down and that we stopped speaking up for what we really believed in.

NO MORE!

Women have something to say. It is time. We are visible and we are creating a wave of voices!

*****

The authors in this book are a group of powerful women leaders who are passionate about leading, serving and making a difference in the world. Kerri in Australia, Marie in Sweden, Yana in Germany, Fiona in western Canada, Karen in Baltimore, Charlene in Chicago, Lynn in Colorado, Brenda in Oregon. In total, twenty-three women who live all over the United States and Canada and around the world.

These twenty-three women initially met through a coaching program including both men and women, and thus were accustomed to "listening" to one another, practicing the artful trade of supporting and empowering others.

Then, we shifted into a new sacred space. For many of us, the process of writing these stories helped us shed a layer of protection that was so worn, it felt like skin. We began to see each other and ourselves more clearly in the journey of writing our stories, building trust and hearing the wisdom that translates from one person's experience to another.

In many of the stories, women wrote about the ways they had been diminished in religion, families, relationships, school, work and the world. Their confidence, feelings of worthiness, personal power, and open-eyed wonder had been chipped away and doused with someone else's fear, manipulation and control. We had turned down the switch to our bright shining lights, to stay safe and hide our power to preserve and protect our hearts.

Sharing our stories with you is the next step in moving so far beyond the insidious "Hey Worthless" that it will hopefully become a notch of completion on our belts. We are carrying our wisdom and strength with us while we leave the rest of the garbage behind.

Here is the Truth: You are amazing. You are beautiful. You are wonderful. Leave the old voices behind in Hitchcock's trailer. Do not look back as you enter this book. Let your intuition guide you to the stories with the exact message you need to hear right now, empowering you even more to reclaim your brilliant light.

Part 1

I AM Power

"Your own words are the bricks and mortar of the dreams you want to realize. Your words are the greatest power you have. The words you choose and their use establish the life you experience."

~Sonia Choquette

Story One

Living My Life as a Question

Adrienne MacDonald

My Life Is As Good As I Allow it to Be. . .

I have always thought that there has to be more to life than what I was living. I felt like maybe there was some rulebook out there that I had not received. Even after I began to allow change and expansion to happen in my life and open up to the opportunities around me, I still knew that something was missing.

That was when I decided to live my life as a question. My **first question** was, **"What might my life look like if I lived my life as a question and answer session?"** I wondered if, just maybe, my life was a question waiting to be revealed. This sounded a little strange to me at first. However, by this time I had read what seemed like every popular self-help book out there. I was a part of many groups and I had truly embraced my new life, as I had moved from the UK to the United States in my early twenties.

My second question was, **"What do I believe is missing in my life?"** When I thought deeply about this and answered the question as truthfully as I could, I realized I felt that what I was missing was a deep connection to myself and possibly God. Just the word God actually sent chills throughout my body. In my head, the word God was this completely loving and accepting energy that was around and inside everything and everyone, as all the new age, self-help books I read said it was. However, in my core I knew I was fooling myself. I didn't feel the love. I felt abandoned and judged by God. It was possible that I no longer even believed in such a deity and I felt scared. I was scared of living and dying, not being good enough, smart enough, thin enough and all the other qualities that I felt that I should be in my mind.

The year was around 1990 and I asked, **"What is my next step? What do I need to do?"** I asked these questions over and over as if they were a prayer. By this time The Oprah Show had become my new favorite show. On one episode she interviewed Marianne Williamson. When I saw this episode it became clear to me that my next step was to read Marianne Williamson's new book: A Return to Love. I could not put this book down once I started it. I even bought it on tape so I could listen to it while I read, as I did not want to miss a single word. This book was changing my life and my vision. It was like food for my soul. This book allowed something to return to me that I did not even know was lost. I felt more inspired and it felt like I was even able to breathe more fully after reading the beautiful words in this now very famous book.

It was now 1993, and my beautiful daughter Kayleen was born. I was amazed and in awe of her. She is perfect in every way imaginable. I could not believe I had been entrusted with someone so small and vulnerable yet so strong. My next questions were, **"How I can be the best Mom for her? What do I need to learn, and where do I find this knowledge? What makes a good parent?"** I recalled mentors I had met and how they had modeled parenting. They showed real compassion and strength and I decided to model after them. Kayleen was so precious it was not long before I was right in the rhythm of being her Mom. I still remember her beautiful sweet smell, her soft skin and baby smile. We just became in sync with each other so easily and before I knew it she changed my life completely. I still do believe that I have learned more from her than she from me.

My next question became, **"Does God Exist?"** When my daughter was around 5 years old I wanted to be able to tell her if there was a higher power. I had started my spiritual journey just a couple of years before she was born, as I had been agnostic for about 15 years before that. I did not want to raise her with a deity or in a religion because I did not want to lie to her. However, I knew by looking at anatomy books and studying the body when I was in nursing school that a human did not create this amazing structure with all its functions, movement and beauty.

I now had learned about and began to believe in vibration, that amazing and perfect flow to life. So I asked, **"God, (I don't remember if I used that actual name) are you real? And what does my daughter need to know about you?"** One thing I did know in my heart was that God is not a person; it is that amazing vibration that is in and around all beings.

Suddenly, I was cocooned in a cloud of love, joy, and amazement with feelings, words and sensations that I did not understand. It fully permeated my whole body through every cell, bone, and muscle. I started to cry, as I did not feel worthy of all this love. However, I had the full memory of the experience and I knew that this is what is real. I was able to tell my daughter that God is this vibration of pure love, and I can tell her this knowing. It is the full truth.

I can still feel that sensation all around me. Even though it is not as intense as it once was, I love that I now feel worthy of that complete and total love. **"Who is God to you?"** Ask the question and find out for yourself.

I continued my question and answer sessions, and some of the questions I asked myself were:

*What would my life look like if I considered myself my own best friend?

*What if my life was filled with so much joy that it would spill over to everyone I met and into everything I did?

*What do I tolerate in others yet judge in myself?

*Why do I have patience for others yet I can be so hard on myself?

*Is this all even possible or was I just being naive?"

Again, I set off on my journey inside of me.

I began to ask **"Will the real me stand UP?"** I took a full inventory of my life from what I was eating to the conversations I was having. I wanted to know who I felt comfortable with and why. I quickly realized that I had a choice everyday; from what I thought about, who I consider a friend, and to find what was and was not working for me.

The answers I received were not always what I wanted to hear at the time, as sometimes the answers were judgments of myself and others. I have always considered myself very down to earth and nonjudgmental and discovering that harsh judgmental side of me was puzzling. I did however discover a very wise me under the layers of judgment and low self-esteem. So, **"How do I allow the wise me to lead?"** became my next question.

I hired a personal trainer to start working out again. A few years before, I hurt my knee in a car accident and I found that I was using my knee pain as an excuse not to exercise. As much as I hated my trainer at times, I knew he had my best interest at heart and was working me to become the best I can be. The workouts felt great and awful all at the same time. I discovered that I was very tenacious and determined which was something I had not recognized in myself before. I would work so hard that I felt legless leaving the gym. Now, I began to see so clearly. I even started looking forward to the workouts and my body began to look and feel healthier.

I decided to invest my time and money into me. I read, I took more classes in alternative medicine like Reiki and energy coaching. I joined Facebook and LinkedIn, I joined a master mind group, made new friends, read new books, and joined Ellie Drake's personal mentoring while continuing to nurse and grow my CPR and first aid business.

I even learned to kayak and took a white water class that I finished by going down a 15-foot waterfall. That river taught me so much about myself that day. I honestly did not think I would be able to finish it. I was scared on the river. The white water kayak was uncomfortable and any time I lost focus the boat spun out of control. Spinning in circles in white water definitely gets your attention. I learned to look forward and come from my core. When my boat rode over that waterfall, I was so proud of myself. I have a picture of myself after the class with my thumbs up next to the white water kayak. It is still my favorite picture of myself.

I realized that my own low self-esteem had held me back long enough. I decided that I would not blame my past or others anymore. My life is mine and I have the power to change anything I needed to. That is true freedom to me. The concept of freedom allowed **my next questions** to arise: **"What was freedom to me? What was my definition of it? And how could I use the concept of freedom to live my life in a way that is true to me?"** So, I wrote my personal rules of freedom and they are listed in no particular order, as each one is important to me:

1. I will save 10% of all my income.
2. I will love more of me always
3. I will have more fun in my life.
4. I will eat food that nourishes me and tastes delicious.
5. I will continue to be a life long learner.
6. I will laugh every day.
7. I will continue to grow my relationship with God.

Now I keep a "Happy Moment's Journal" for the times when I cannot feel gratitude. I can always pick at least one happy moment on that day or time in my life. So, when I feel really stuck, I will ask myself, **"What are the happy moments that I can remember?"**, and I write them down. I find these happy moments raise my vibration and lead me to feelings of expectancy and gratitude.

I invite you to take an inventory of your life. Just pick one piece and question it. **"What are you eating?"** List it on paper, and don't over think it, because if you are anything like me, you'll gloss over some of the things on your list if you do. **Ask yourself; is this food healthy for me?** If you have listed 5 days of fast food then maybe the food is not healthy. **Ask yourself, "Do I want to change this?"** Remember, this is your life. So if the answer is "no" then continue eating as you please. Enjoy it...every bite! Even lick the plate if you want to.

If the answer is **"yes"** then ask yourself, **"When do I want to start these changes and why?"** Do it for you!

Write reminders about the changes you are making. I have lots of reminders. One of my favorite reminders is to use index cards or blank bookmarks and place them in books that I am reading.

Each one of us was born to thrive. My daughter has a silver question mark on her bedroom wall that reads, **"Question Everything."** I bought this for her when she was four years old and I use it as a reminder to have her live her life as a question.

Recently, I have been studying with Rikka Zimmerman from Access Consciousness work. It surprised me when I learned the program is about asking even more questions. This feels very right to me and I definitely know my life is being enhanced.

Asking questions has been my journey as a natural intuitive and I have found me. I have grown and added to my long list of certifications, with Vibrational Life Coach, Energy Coach, Teen Coach and Access BARS Facilitator.

Ending this story with a few questions feels appropriate.

"How amazing can you truly be?"

"What is great about you that you're not seeing?"

My hope is that I have enticed you to ask questions. After all this is your life. Will questions change your life?

My guess is they will.

Adrienne MacDonald *is a natural intuitive coach and believes that you are "THE GIFT" you have been waiting for. The first love affair is with yourself while allowing others to enhance you. You are here to be the "best" that you are so you can bring out the best in others. She is the founder of CPR and Safety, The Gift of Focus and Everything is Vibration/Empaths Academy. She moved from the United Kingdom to the United States by herself in her early twenty's after growing up in the war in Belfast, Northern Ireland and was seeking change. She is a US citizen that lived in the UK.*

Adrienne lives in GA with her husband Edward of 25 years and her daughter Kayleen. Her joy is showing people their unique beauty, and empowering plus bringing the spirit of collaboration to groups.

To contact Adrienne www.thegiftoffocus.com
www.cprsafety.com www.everythingisvibration.com

Story Two

Finding Me

Kerri Jones

Just before my daughter turned one, I fell sick. At the time we didn't know what was wrong. I felt exhausted, hopeless and sad. I could not "get going"; everything was an effort. I lost my spark, my joie de vivre. I was very teary. I remember sitting on the couch most days, crying. I didn't know why I was crying, but the tears still flowed. I hoped my daughter would not remember me on the couch crying! I felt like a bad mother, a failure. I knew there was something wrong, I just did not know what.

I was 37 years old and at home with my first baby. I had been an independent woman until now. I had been married for just three years. My husband and I allowed a lot of space in our relationship for being individuals. We really honored each other's needs and supported the pursuit of our respective passions.

We had moved from Sydney to the country when we were married, three years previously. We commuted together to Sydney for work, where we stayed over most weeks to cut down on the travelling. So this was my first year living full-time in a rural area. I am a city girl at heart. Even though I do love the peace and beauty of where we live, it was a huge adjustment for me. I really missed my family and my friends and the conveniences and familiarity of the city. We had no electricity, instead a noisy generator! I could write a whole story about life with a generator! We lived half an hour from the nearest supermarket, there were no playgrounds and I didn't know anyone, except for a wonderful elderly neighbor who was my lifeline.

Becoming a mother was also a huge adjustment. I loved my daughter deeply and appreciated a lot about my new life. Around the time I fell ill, I was still breastfeeding and recovering on some levels from my daughter's birth, which had really claimed my energy and knocked my confidence. I had a very long delivery and for months after felt very disappointed about the way I delivered. When the obstetrician was tending to me shortly after the birth, he made the comment "I'm going to sew you up nice and tight for your husband." I was pretty whacked from the delivery and was so shocked by his statement no words came. I was speechless. I slipped into victim mode. Sadly his "sewing" has caused me great discomfort over the years, which has also had a huge impact on our sex life.

However, the most challenging thing of all was, I missed my husband. I longed for his presence during this difficult time of adjustment and I desperately wanted to spend quality time as a little family. He was busy working five days a week to support us. It was my decision to be a stay at home Mum and he supported me. I was keen to get back to some part-time work in the near future. As it happens…divine timing…he was also building our house next door, on weekends! I knew that he wanted to build us a home when we got married. It was a passion, which he had always dreamed of, and he threw his heart and soul into it. In hindsight it was just the timing that was tricky! However, I felt abandoned and a victim of circumstance. This was the time in my life I MOST needed him. For the first time in my life I felt really lonely. He was totally preoccupied with all his responsibilities…so I got sick!

Looking back now I know that I became ill in an attempt to get his attention, or anyone's! Mum suggested I give up breastfeeding, which I did and it really helped me to regain some of my physical strength and independence. By the time I found out that I had had glandular fever, the first bout was over and I was beginning to realize that I had moved into depression. It was probably undiagnosed post-natal depression. I was a naturalist so it never occurred to me to seek medication. To be honest, anything would have been better than the deep dark place I went to, for way too long.

When my daughter was six months old, I joined the local Mothers Group and began to meet and make friends. To this day I have a truly wonderful and lifesaving group of local friends who I am deeply grateful for. I remember one friend in particular on many occasions saying, "Kerri, you just have to pack up the baby and get out of the house. You have to make yourself go out!"

For the 5-6 years that my husband was building our house on weekends, I felt really alone. I was missing my mate, my spiritual partner. My spiritual cup felt empty. My husband begged me to spend more time at the house with him, to bring our daughter over and be together. We spent some time there, but I found having a toddler at a building site stressful and unrelaxing. I injured my back when my daughter was two years old, so I was unable to physically contribute. He was building a timber slab house, so the materials were heavy and out of my league. My resentment was deep. I took the victim stance and blamed him and the house for all my problems and for my unhappiness. I saw the house and his obsession with it as the culprit! It was this resistance to my situation, which kept me stuck for so long!

I had gone back to some part-time massage work and swimming instruction. I loved both these expressions of me! Injuring my back also meant I had to give up my work as a massage therapist. I was really passionate about massage and healing. I just loved it. It really crushed me when I had to give it away. I so missed the work and making a contribution to people's lives. I searched for another healing modality for years. However, nothing was a fit. I was looking for a modality that would not challenge me physically, as a practitioner. In hindsight it just wasn't the right time for me. I felt gutted and my life lacked passion now. Except for my daughter, who was a constant light, albeit a challenging one at times!!

A few years later I had to give up swimming instruction as well. My daughter was allergic to the chlorine & I was having a lot of problems now with my skin, related to the chlorine and the sun! I went on to find other part-time work, but nothing else really "lit" me up the way massage and swim teaching did.

In the background of all the day-to-day drudgery, we were trying to conceive. My body clock was ticking, as I was now 39 years old. I fell pregnant again and we were thrilled. I felt really strongly about having a sibling for my daughter and my husband would have had six babies if I had agreed!! Very sadly, I miscarried around my daughter's third birthday. I knew the pregnancy wasn't right but it was still a huge blow. Looking back I did not grieve sufficiently. I'd had a miscarriage before my daughter, which only compounded this loss. We continued to try for another baby for about 4-5 long years.

During this time I really questioned our marriage and whether bringing another baby into such an uncertain relationship was fair. I had lost my confidence in our marriage. Trying to conceive undermined any spontaneity in our sex life and was emotionally exhausting. The only reason we continued was because of my age....we were running out of time! Everyone around us was falling pregnant again. It was difficult. Yet at the same time we were filled with gratitude that we had our beautiful daughter.

My heart goes out to women who are unable to conceive, it is a deeply saddening experience. I felt really useless as a woman, that I was unable to fall pregnant again and give my husband the gift of another child. He loves children and they love him. Even more sadly, I desperately wanted my daughter to have a sibling. I have three wonderful sisters and I hoped my daughter would experience a brother or a sister.

At some point we found out that I had endometriosis, so I had an operation to remove this and then there was another opportunity to fall pregnant. I never fell pregnant again. We gave the idea up when I was about 44 years old. Ever since then I have been experiencing debilitating migraines!

I felt stripped…I lost my health, my joy, my husband (to the house), my work, my passion, pregnancies, the ability to conceive and most painfully I lost myself. Things weren't going well! It was difficult to watch my husband living his dream, being on purpose and not to feel resentful. I felt trapped by circumstances, a victim with no real idea of how to break free. I continued to resist, I could not accept my situation. I felt I was living his dream, not mine.

When our daughter was about six years old my husband's time was finally freed up on weekends. We had moved into our house two years previously, despite it being a long way from finished. I was starting to pull out of the depression and for me there was now a gaping hole in our relationship. For the past six years, I had spent most weekends with just my daughter. Opportunities were coming up now for us as a couple to reconnect, but I just wasn't that interested. I wasn't that interested in anything! I had left the marriage mentally and spiritually. I was far away from him and I did not know how to get back or if I wanted to. And I was far away from me. I was deeply unhappy. I found it really hard to feel love for him again. This really saddened us both and I felt so much guilt, which I just had to sit with. He was still deeply in love with me, but a whole part of me had closed down and I did not know if or how I could open up again.

My unhappiness had me wondering whether this was the right relationship for me. My libido was very low, as I now found myself in perimenopause! This brought a whole new set of symptoms and difficulties, including the migraines. There were many occasions I would have liked to run far, far away. I did know though, on some level, that by running I would only be taking the problems with me!! After all, I was the one experiencing the problems, not my husband. This of course fed one of my core beliefs "I'm not good enough"! I was constantly comparing myself to my husband, who time & again assured me he was happy. I had to own the fact that it was me who was disconnected, discontent & unhappy.

On September 11th 2001 it was our 8th wedding anniversary. For us at this time there was not much to celebrate. When news came through of the terrible tragedy in New York, I was stunned by this powerful analogy. I realized the tragedy in my own life. It felt like our marriage had been blown apart.

Not long after I made a friend with whom I had a strong spiritual connection. Through her I learned some very powerful and painful lessons. I also found myself in a circle of warm and loving women, with whom I had fun! When I reflect on this group I immediately smile, inside and out! However, I was still unhappy. I questioned myself a lot. I began to party hard, an old pattern that resurfaced. I became self-destructive. This impacted heavily on my husband and my daughter. During this time I failed my husband, my daughter and myself. This behavior ostracized me further from myself. What began as a spiritual connection had me travelling in a whole other direction and that was… away from me! It took me a few years to recognize where I was at and that I needed to STOP. This was an intensely painful period for us all, but it also produced miracles! It was about now that I hit absolute rock bottom. I had to do something, anything! I had been here before, I knew exactly what to do…I had to get sober; I had to face my reality!

So we took our first family holiday and went to Fiji. Our daughter was seven years old and this holiday was a turning point for us as a couple and a family. We had quality time together and it felt wonderful! Just the three of us in a beautiful place, supported by friendly Fijians & a Kids Club! Our daughter had fun and we reconnected as a couple. We celebrated our 10th wedding anniversary there & my husband surprised me at dinner with a candle lit cake carried by a group of Fijians singing "Happy Anniversary"! We all treasure this holiday & our time there together.

Our experience in Fiji gave me hope for the future. Change wasn't immediate, but eventually we were able to turn our marriage around and move forward slowly together.

One major thing we had going for us, was that we wanted to stay together. So we dug deep! We tried counseling for a while and did a course for couples. We had an open line of communication. I was able to communicate my feelings, even though this was painful for us both. We had strong family support on both sides and I am deeply grateful to my sisters and my friends for their love and light. One friend in particular was a shining example for me throughout these dark years.

I had to dig very deep. I remembered back to how we were as a couple in the beginning. I found photos that reminded me of how happy we were. We did have great energy together, so I believed we could again! I thought about all the qualities in my husband that I had admired. Why I fell in love with him and the confidence I felt when I chose him. And I did wonder…"how the hell did we end up here"? It was such a shock; I had never imagined that this could happen to us!

I looked around for role models and found three couples close to us that I both loved and admired. I noticed the qualities they had as couples, qualities that we could emulate. What stood out with all three couples was they laughed together. They were able to laugh at themselves and to see the humor in life and everything it threw at them. I noticed that we hardly laughed when we were together. I noticed how serious and heavy we had become. I was up for change. This is where I sourced my inspiration. I believed we had what it took. I clung to this belief.

I was still unhappy within myself, my purpose was unclear and I felt lost. I longed for a career I felt passionate about. Health problems continued to plague me, in particular the migraines. Finally in 2010, I came across a radio show and a couple, Kristin and David Morelli who would help me change my life. I joined their program, **The Immersion Solution,** and it was during this program I became aware again of my purpose. I was reminded of my passion for healing and my desire to serve and support others. I had forgotten who I was! It was time to give back. This insight turned my life around.

I joined their Enwaken Coaching program and for the first time in many years I felt excited and passionate. This energy coaching work was exactly what I had been looking for and I was more than ready!! I found myself amongst a group of wonderful, like-minded folk, who were committed to transformation. Participating in this course gave me back to me! It was an absolute gift and it allowed me to transform my life and myself. This energy work has affected all areas of my life, including my health and my marriage. I no longer feel depressed, anxious or live in constant fear.

My mind is quieter, my life has been simplified. I am a better wife and mother, a happier and more content woman. I love my work and I am excited about my future!

My husband and I have been together for 18 years; my daughter is 15 years old. Our marriage is still evolving. Our house is still evolving. I am still evolving! Alcohol is no longer a part of my life. Slowly, slowly we have built a bridge back to one another.

I do not know what the future holds, but I do know that I am profoundly blessed by having these two people in my life and deeply grateful for their love.

I am especially grateful for finding me!

Kerri Jones *lives with her family in Australia, in a rural area north of Sydney. She is an Intuitive Life Coach, a Simply Healed practitioner, a trained teacher and healer. Kerri is passionate about personal transformation, spirituality, yoga, health and fitness. She loves travel, nature, outdoor pursuits and spending time with family & friends. Through this Book Project, Kerri has rediscovered the joy of writing and is inspired to begin a blog. As her mission evolves, she sees herself supporting and guiding others, particularly women, as they each transform their lives and move towards their goals.*
Kerri can be found on Facebook and LinkedIn.
kjwildwood@bigpond.com

Story Three

Choice

Sandy Kobruck

February 12 is the day my husband and I celebrate our anniversary - the night 27 years ago when we acknowledged the truth we'd been denying for months because that truth was neither convenient nor popular. It was an excellent choice. For those 27 years, we have shared adventures while working in and exploring the mountains of the West. Our appreciation and love for one another has grown as we each walked our own path while believing in and supporting the other. We chose with our hearts. For most of that time, we have not heard the tick...tick...tick....

Three days after this year's anniversary we were skiing the local backcountry in southern Colorado along the

Continental Divide. As we made our way down the mountain, I suddenly initiated and was caught in an avalanche. The small tree immediately below me arrested my progress and I felt the 3-foot deep snow mass flow around me and down the slope. In that moment I wasn't scared. I was, however, completely present, intensely aware of the choices I needed to make in the instant the snow began to slide underneath me. I can recall my thoughts, feelings and actions in each second...tick...tick...tick...

The following day three men set a much larger avalanche in motion on a forested mountain slope a mile away from my avalanche. All three were engulfed in the moving snow. Amazingly, two of them were only partially buried. For one, an encounter with a tree extracted several teeth in exchange for his life. The second was buried to his waist as he skied desperately out of the way of the thundering snow. The third was buried six feet deep in the snow, wrapped around a large spruce tree.   His two friends were forced to rescue themselves before turning their attention to their buried friend. It takes a long time to dig through six feet of rock hard avalanche debris, even if you are young and strong. Tick...tick...tick... He suffocated as his two friends worked desperately to reach him and dig him out.

Mirella, my best friend, recently found out she has a brain cyst. It's been growing for 7 years, undetected until this week. No one connected her numb face to a cyst expanding in her brain. She isn't sure what action she should choose. Surgery involves serious risks. It appears to be a slow-growing tumor, so perhaps she has some time to decide.   She hears the...tick...tick...tick...

Last week Mirella said to me, "I am looking at my life and asking, 'what did I do that contributed to a cyst growing in my brain?' Did toxic pollutants or other external factors contribute? Perhaps. But, you know, I believe that my thoughts, my feelings, my actions, the stories I tell myself that excuse my thoughts and actions, these choices I make consciously and unconsciously that don't serve me, I believe they have also contributed. Things I do that are not aligned with my joy, my brilliance, and my freedom. We do so many things in our lives that don't serve us. We live shallow lives spending our precious energy on things that really don't matter, that don't connect us deeply to our true self. "

In that moment I saw that 90% of the things I chose to do, say, be, and think in my life don't serve me. My actions often don't bring me closer to happiness and peace, satisfaction and appreciation, joy and laughter, which is truly our birthright. So often I don't make choices that support me in shining my light, my gifts, my magnificence into the world. I saw it so clearly - 90% of my life I am totally getting in my own way. I choose to think, feel, and act in ways that move me in the opposite direction of what I want, of who I truly am at my deepest core. As a result my life feels foggy, congested, and mis-focused.

This week I came face to face with how much life can change in a few seconds: the importance of honoring deep feelings of love, being caught in an avalanche, discovering a tumor. As an Essence life coach, I receive the gift of seeing people's clarity, lightness, and newfound freedom as their deep blocks shift. It feels like magic each time, yet it is real. Limits come off; the energy is allowed to rise up, to expand, to move out as they connect to their true self. They choose to look into the places most people fear, and their life shifts.

Before her MRI an intuitive naturopath performed an energetic reading of Mirella's brain that was as accurate as the subsequent MRI. When Mirella recounted this to me I said, "I would love to be able to read energy that accurately and clearly." Her retort stopped me in my tracks, as I felt its resonant truth. "You can, Sandy. You choose your limiting beliefs. If you choose to believe that you have access to that same clarity of information, then you engage your potential. If you choose to believe you aren't that talented, then you cripple the possibility. Choose differently. In truth, you are the only one who can."

As I write this the preciousness of each moment presses poignantly against me. Tick…tick…tick…tick…

For a moment imagine your life as a child's toy block. The volume of the block represents all your thoughts, your actions, your beliefs, and your emotions. The way most of us live our lives, this block is almost completely filled with thoughts, emotions, and actions, beliefs that divorce us from our dreams, our happiness, and our success. In the toy's far upper corner occupying the tiniest space is the area representing our actions, thoughts, and beliefs that align with our true, brilliant selves, where we believe in ourselves, where we are directly connected to our divinity. So often aligned, connected actions occupy only a small portion of our day. We think we are doing the "right thing", but in reality we are our own worst enemy.

I don't want death to be the sole reminder to bring awareness and gratitude in each moment. I can choose to pay attention, to be present. I can ask, "What is it I am choosing right now?" I can choose to be gentle with myself and others. I can choose to notice when I impose limiting beliefs - and make a different choice. To notice when I choose acceptance not judgment, to laugh not scowl, to receive not rebuff. To fill my toy block with belief in my brilliance, with laugh-out-loud joy, with ease, awareness, and love.

Tick...tick...tick...

I can make that choice.

Sandy Kobruck *is a life long avalanche professional. She operates The Wolf Creek Avalanche School in southwestern Colorado. Sandy runs a mountain hut on the Continental Divide in Colorado and offers multi-day skiing, mountain biking, trail running, and hiking excursions. In her transformational coaching business Sandy integrates exciting worldwide adventures with accelerated energy coaching techniques. Contact Sandy: sandykobrock@gmail.com*

Story Four

From Darkness Into the Light

Lynn Wertheimer

"There was a little girl who had a little curl right in the middle of her forehead. When she was good she was very, very good, but when she was bad she was horrid."

The meaning I associated with that childhood rhyme is that I was horrid. It was etched into my psyche because I can only recall my mom reciting this rhyme to me when I was bad in order to influence me to behave like a good little girl.

The little girl inside me took this feeling bad to heart and started beating up on myself for being less than perfect. It is not unusual for us to compare ourselves with others. Somehow I took it to a very low level.

My sense of self worth got so low during my teenage years that I had an acronym for myself, POS. It meant Piece of Shit. I even carved those letters on the side of the drawer of my nightstand in my bedroom. When I opened that drawer those letters, POS served as a constant reminder of my worthlessness and pain I was feeling about myself.

In high school, I don't know how I functioned as an A minus student with that amount of self-loathing. My rebelliousness emerged at the National Honor Society's induction ceremony where I wore a black armband on the outside of my gray graduation robe that said, "Stop the Killing." The year was 1970 and this was shortly after the Kent State killings.

I had few friends. The friends I did have I compared myself to unfavorably. I felt fat and ugly. I rarely dated. I felt isolated, lonely, disconnected and depressed. I stayed alone in my bedroom a lot listening to music on WLS AM radio in Chicago. The songs that reinforced my melancholy moods were songs like "I am a Rock" and "Eleanor Rigby" "All the lonely people where do they all belong?" I was lonely and wondering where I belonged. I hated myself intensely. I identified with lyrics like "you expect for me to love you when you hate yourself my friend." How could anyone love me when I was radiating such self-hatred? I felt empty and darkness inside.

Being a baby boomer, I was drawn towards using recreational drugs. Eventually drugs went beyond fun and partying and drew me into myself, into that darkness that seemed safe. That isolation became my comfort zone.

No one could criticize me more harshly than I could criticize myself. Criticizing myself was a regular habit. I was dysfunctional with the few friends I did have. I would give to others and not ask for myself until I would inappropriately explode in anger and upset. It felt like a nosedive into a cesspool of self-pity.

Boyfriends or even dates were few and far between. When I did get the attention of a man named Larry I was uncomfortable with the attention I received. I felt resistant to being loved and afraid of disapproval from my family. One night before a planned vacation I totaled my car. My friend and I took that trip to Colorado where I fell in love with the mountains all over again.

I felt like the mountains called to me. When I was a little girl during many summers I visited my grandmother in Tucson, which is surrounded by beautiful mountains. After my trip to Colorado in 1977, I moved to Tucson thinking I finally had all the pieces of the success puzzle, a college degree and work experience. Surely I would easily find a job, but I was wrong. My low self-esteem was causing me to feel like I was spiraling down.

My journey eventually took me to the Grand Canyon where I worked as a waitress instead of continuing in the new field I worked as a paralegal. After my initial three-month work commitment, I drove up the coast of California with a friend.

My intention was to return to the Midwest after my trip up the coast and reconnect with my boyfriend, Larry. What happened next was the start of a deep dark period for me. After going drinking with friends at a bar, called Mothers, we returned to a "house in the shade of the freeway" (just like the lyrics from Jackson Browne's song, "The Pretender"). This house was where we had many parties when I previously lived there. Some friends and I had partied all day without Larry because he was off visiting another woman he had been dating while I was out west. After our walk to that house from the bar I went into one of the bedrooms and passed out on the bed.

What happened next was like a surreal nightmare. I didn't hear the party in the next room. I didn't hear the house being broken into by a gang of three men who were holding up homes in the Drake University area. I didn't hear the gunshot that sent a bullet into Larry's throat when he stood up to these men. I woke up when my pants were being taken off me and one of the robbers entered me and started to rape me. Because of my alcohol consumption I vomited and he left me alone. I was taken to one hospital and Larry to another hospital. This was before paramedics and advanced medical equipment, so Larry died that night.

I was staying at the house where Larry lived with his sister and her family. The cops came there to ask me more questions. They insisted I was a liar because they found drugs and paraphernalia in the backyard of the house where the

shooting happened.   The cops then arrested me for being
uncooperative as a material witness. They handcuffed me and
took me to jail barefoot. I remember crying in the squad car on
the way to jail.

This shooting of Larry and rape happened in the city
where I had previously worked as a paralegal. I called one of
the attorneys I used to work with to help me. He came to my
rescue. I recall standing up to the cops when they asked me to
take a lie detector test. In that moment of being challenged, I
found strength as well as tapped into lessons I learned from
an assertive defense class so my response was, "Because I
prefer not to." After the cops released me, the attorney drove
me to Larry's sister's house in his Mercedes convertible.

Larry's funeral was more of a party than a solemn
occasion. They played his favorite songs: Take it to the Limit
and A Place in the Sun. After the church service we smoked
his pot and drank beer from a keg.

What made me decide to return to the Grand Canyon
and withdraw from my family was being blamed for the rape
by my parents. This happened in August 1978.

By December of that same year, I found out my dad
had pneumonia…but, it wasn't pneumonia. It was lung
cancer. I was working again at the Grand Canyon. I saw him
in February of 1979 in Tucson for my grandmother's 75th
birthday. It shocked me how thin and weak he had become.
Then I got the call from my family at work - "You need to
come back now." So back to the Midwest I went and arrived a
day before he died in April 1979. I felt like my dad waited for
me. He didn't speak to acknowledge me verbally, but I knew
that he knew I was there.

Two trips back to the Midwest and two men I cared for
and loved had died. I felt like a jinx that caused those deaths.
I returned to the Grand Canyon again. I self medicated on
drugs to numb out and hiked to escape the pain. I would talk
to my dad's spirit on those hikes.

Fast forward to living in Northern California then back
to Arizona. I was still isolated and living alone with my cats
most of the time. In Tucson, there was another boyfriend
named Larry. I recognized the victim energy in me attracted

the victim energy in him. I put up with Larry's verbal abuse until my male cat, Avee (Ah-vee) started licking fur off his body and making himself bald. My cat was giving me the message to leave. This Larry died in front of me from a heart attack and then was revived by paramedics. My decision to leave Larry and Tucson was already made and I had the courage to hold firm and leave.

Many times during my teenage years and adult years when I was living alone I felt deep pain and had suicidal thoughts. I cried. I had the kind of pity parties you don't send out any invitations for others to join. Because I lived alone and isolated myself I felt like I wouldn't be missed if I terminated my life. What stopped me from acting on my suicidal thoughts was a commitment I made to my cats to care for them for their entire life after feeling guilty for leaving one of my cats in the Midwest. Their love for me and my love for them pulled me through, but did not end the pain.

Last year during energy coaching training I was surprised to learn that my essence was a bright light. How can that be? I still experienced myself as darkness. Why were the other coaching students having breakthroughs and not me? Why did I still feel so low and have suicidal thoughts even after releasing blocks with all the energy work? Was it because I took on others' dark energies when I healed others unconsciously? At times I had thoughts of throwing myself in front of the train. Other times I cried and called out to God to take me out.

A note I sent to unemployment after they put a hold on my benefits stated I was seriously suicidal even though in that moment I really wasn't. This was my own episode of "Girl Interrupted." The sheriff came and took me away again in handcuffs, this time to the emergency room.

Somehow I had a sense that this was a gift even as my freedom was temporarily taken away. Finally I was getting help. I realized I had been depressed for years. It is still a healing process. My brothers and mom rallied around me. I received love and caring support from some of my coaching friends. I am so grateful to all of them.

This has been a turning point for me. I am no longer living alone. I am getting medical and counseling help as well as using energy healing practices. My coaching buddy suggested I turn on the light inside me. It helps me keep an awareness of the light my coaching friends see in my essence. I am beginning to feel lighter.

Since then I have thrived at my seasonal job. I am doing what I love connecting to people using my analytical and intuitive skills. Some clients even mentioned they liked my energy, which is a wonderful validation. I noticed I feel more in flow in work as well as driving in traffic. What I discovered is I have an ability to see patterns with finances where I can advise my clients. My problem solving skills have improved. I recognize a growing joy and confidence inside me.

Recently I experienced an increasing sense of my personal strength and power. A friend's situation occurred where I came to her side when the cops thought she was impaired like she appeared to be drunk and I knew and believed she wasn't. I wrote a letter to her boss. I was proved right after medical tests revealed it was a seizure condition. I value her friendship and this experience.

Now I see I do matter and I would be missed by more than my cats. I have emerged from the darkness of isolation into the light, shining brightly.

It is still a choice and sometimes a challenge for me to choose the light instead of darkness. Now I am more aware when I return to that familiar vibration of darkness because it feels heavy. When I am feeling light that feels good.

Now…I wonder…what else is possible?

*Lynn Wertheimer comes from the Midwest, a third generation first born female who has five awesome brothers. She is compiling her mom and grandma's recipes for a dynamic cookbook. She now lives in the Greater Denver area with her two cats and works as a seasonal tax preparer. She loves connecting with her clients using her analytical and intuitive skills advising from the heart. Lynn has a passion for spiritual and healing practices including dowsing, energy readings. You can contact Lynn at **lynnw2810@gmail.com** and visit her site at **http://www.lynnwertheimer.com**. Lynn asks that we always recognize we have a light inside and remember to turn on the switch whenever it seems dark.*

Story Five

The Power of Self:
When You Believe...All In

Cathi Ketterling

My life has truly felt like a journey. From a young age, I was always excited as one chapter ended and a new one began. Of course it was not always smooth and easy, it was sometimes sad and bumpy. Somehow, I always landed on my feet stepping forward.

Fast forward from high school to college. I applied for pharmacy school during my sophomore year not even realizing that I would first have to be accepted. As I read my acceptance letter, I did not even give thought to how many had applied and were turned away. When they say ignorance is bliss, I think there could be some truth in that statement. I attended college feeling like I must have been pretty lucky.

Honestly, thinking back on it, failure didn't even exist. No one had ever told me that failure could have been a possibility. I started and finished with the mindset of I am going to become a pharmacist and that was that.

It is amazing to look back at it all and to deconstruct it. No layering of failure, fear, or self-doubt had occurred. Just pure passion as I pursued the path I was choosing for my life. It was almost child-like as all I saw were options and possibilities. As I sit here and write, I take a deep breath going back to that place and energetically re-living it in my mind. It was pure spirit in action.

So what the heck happened? You know, life goes on and the pace keeps getting faster and faster. Then when all my friends started graduating from college I started to unconsciously play the keeping up with the Jones' games. We were all upgrading our homes, cars, clothes, and spending nearly everything we made. It is a world I was easily sucked into and before I knew it what I earned was never enough. I was a higher income earner so I dove off the high dive into a high consumption lifestyle that was quickly consuming my soul.

For many years I pushed myself harder and harder and found myself in the entrepreneurial world. For the first few years it was great. My husband and I bought our first pharmacy with no money down. Basically we bought it with our great reputations. We bought the second pharmacy nearly the same way and started our 3rd business from scratch. Our income had quadrupled which ended up feeding the monster I had created with even more financial resources. I was working 60+ hours per week and trading my soul for material things.

During this time I found a mentor named Bob Proctor. I noticed that I would get pretty run down and nearly depressed, especially during the wintertime. I am sure a lack of sunshine, living in the Northern hemisphere, had something to do with it. But, it was very noticeable and uncomfortable and I could not spend my way out of those blues. Bob taught me about mindset and how it can sabotage you. I also became aware of my ego and how it was running my life more than I was. I was fully out of control with this lifestyle and somehow knew I couldn't keep this up for much longer. My physical body was starting to weaken and I could feel how unhealthy this lifestyle was. You can only deplete yourself for so long and I had used up all of my body's natural resources.

Bob was my first stepping-stone into the self-help world and I will be forever grateful for that. He opened my eyes to a whole new world. That world was possibility. It became possible once again to create the life I had always wanted by simply using my mind. Yes, it all starts somewhere and when you create something in your mind, then you can create it in your reality.

Now, this is the point where a lot of people get to which is totally fine. They find a self-help guru and learn to meditate, go to seminars, chant, or whatever else from an endless list of activities. Don't get me wrong; I am not criticizing any of these practices. I have learned many skills, which I still use today, but these activities can only help you go so far. After a while you notice your old patterns returning, sabotaging any remnant of success you seem to be gaining. As I made more money, I spent more money. It happened unconsciously. I actually didn't even realize I had created giant leaky holes in my wealth and in my health.

I started noticing how stressed out I had become. Gaining weight, poor sleep at night, and just a mess in general. I believe my adrenals were burning out. I could go from happy to off the handle in about 3 seconds and I didn't know why. I only knew that something had to change quickly so I didn't end up with a serious illness or in a mental hospital.

During this stressful time of my life I had the privilege of taking an immersion course called, **40 Days and 40 Nights to a Quantum Leap in Your Wealth.** I found the program on Facebook. It just appeared! It is awesome how things show up when you are just surfing sites like this. This is how my life suddenly took a huge turn. I followed this 40-day program to the letter. I was on every call, did every assignment, and wrote in my journal, set my goals. Everything. I remember setting this huge, scary goal of selling one of my businesses by the completion of the 40 days. Well, day 40 rolled around and I did have my business listed, but so far no offers. I was disappointed to say the least, but one of the principles I had learned was to set audacious goals and take steps towards those goals one-step at a time. I was doing that, but I still felt a bit devastated deep down inside.

At that point, all I could do was feel the devastation and keep working toward my goal. As I worked through this using the energy tools I had learned, I found that I was not devastated at all and that I had a renewed feeling towards my pharmacies. My husband and I started doing everything we could to make our businesses rock! I won't get into all of those types of details, but we were pouring our hearts and souls into making these businesses the best they could be.

During this time of working on our businesses, I received a call from a competing business owner who wanted to set up a meeting. I said yes as I was curious as to why he had called. During this meeting, he mentioned that I had three businesses in the same towns that he also had three businesses. After the meeting, I simply told him I was not interested. My main pharmacy was competing with one of his pharmacies and we were kicking their pants and I was really proud of that.

About three months later I found a new broker for my pharmacy. Not long after hiring this new company, he had a lead. This lead not only wanted to purchase one pharmacy, they wanted all three. As it happened, it was the same guy I had met with three months earlier. Sometimes you almost have to be hit over the head to realize it was right in front of you all along. As soon as he told me who our potential buyer was, I instantly knew this was it.

On the anniversary of the 40 Days and 40 Nights program I had sold all three of my businesses to a single buyer for cash in an economy that had taken a beating. The sale only took two months and it was absolutely flawless.

The sale of those businesses opened up the door for me to find a career path that was more in alignment with my true essence. I had been searching for my true essence all along and little did I know for a long time it is my soul and has always been with me. My true essence was under the shadow of years of energetic baggage I had accumulated. I enrolled in a life-coaching program that incorporated the use of reading, seeing, and healing energy. This was an absolutely 100% different type of training for me to get involved with. Somehow I knew it was just where I needed to be. Over the yearlong training I learned so much about how to raise my own vibration, attract what I want in life, and to help others do the same. I also found an awesome way to use my pharmacy degree as well. I found an amazing medical school that offers a masters program in anti-aging and functional medicine. I have always had a passion for phenomenal health and I knew pushing prescriptions toward people was not the answer.

I look back now and love where I am going in my life. I am armed with tools to help people live the best life they can live both in their physical health and their regular lives. We are not as helpless or hopeless as so many people in the world seem. There is a whole quantum energetic field that we are all a part of that with a little training can help us live the lives we were meant to live.

Cathi Ketterling *was born and raised in Rupert, Idaho. She attended college at Idaho State University in Pocatello, Idaho to pursue a career in Pharmacy. Cathi now lives with her husband and kitty in Twin Falls, Idaho for the past 17 years.*

After college Cathi started working as a pharmacist at Sav-Mor Drug in Buhl, Idaho. A few years later she and her husband bought that pharmacy. Over the following few years they bought a pharmacy in Ely, Nevada and opened another in Star, Idaho. After 8 great awesome entrepreneurial years, Cathi sold all 3 pharmacies to pursue a career in life coaching and Anti-Aging health consulting. **Cathiketterling@ymail.com** **www.facebook.com/cathi.ketterling** **www.twitter.com/cathik**

Story Six

Waking Up

Elizabeth Love

Sobs I can't control wrench my body, making it hard to see the trees and plowed fields rolling past the windshield.

Every time I drive alone the anguish jumps me, like a delinquent, lurking in a parking lot.

The keening... howling... I don't recognize my own voice. What the hell is going on?

The car is my only place of solitude, and rarely even then; without my boys, without my husband, without the responsibilities of the house and farm. Am I going crazy? I don't even know why I'm at the edge of my life - my normal, good life - hemorrhaging grief.

Only that this, somehow, is the most honest I've ever allowed myself to be.

And that thought terrifies me.

It all started as an innocent whisper, a faint scent on the breeze - the coming of spring that beckons wintering birds to

renounce their exile and wing their way home.
It didn't start as grief... but a stirring.

Waking up.

How long have I been sleeping?

Why is it so hard to remember the past 20 years?

Halley. My mare. Trust an alpha mare to wake a woman up! She is the fruition of a lifelong dream.

We bought the farmhouse. Built the stalls, cleared and fenced the pastures and rings, built the hay shed, the hitching post, and after 39 years of longing, of lessons and leasing, of working as groom, trainer, instructor in others' barns, I brought home Halley, my first horse.

I can't stop the grin, as I picture pointing my finger at her. "She started it!" I didn't mean for it to go here.

I just wanted to have my own horse.

But she taught me the dance of her language... body, focus, energy, movement, emotion, congruence. She was my Rosetta Stone, taking me from the world of riding, jumping, training, showing - and initiating me into a world of energetic connection - teaching me to whisper with her.

All the while, bringing me back to my native tongue.
... that first scent of fertile ground opening to the sun.

It's dangerous to wake up. To remember who I am.

Like the recurring dreams I have each month - have had for over a decade, of a tidal wave eclipsing the beach I'm standing on, swallowing people, buildings, cars... everything in its path. And there's no escape. I'm running and running, but it roars over me, over everyone around me, bringing total destruction - and I wake up shaking, gasping for breath.

I love the ocean.

But there's something in those depths that will consume me. Consume the life I've built.

What have I built?

Over 20 years of marriage to a good man; Two fantastic boys - homeschooled for years, and now happily enrolled in a local charter school. My farm, my horses...

So why do I get hives every night before my husband comes home?

Why does he get up in the middle of the night, every night, to sleep till morning on the couch?

I'm haunted by the recurring dream that he walks up to me and tells me he never loved me, and doesn't want to be married to me anymore... I watch helpless, as my life crumbles around me, and he walks off, indifferent.
With each dream, because they happen so often, I'm convinced that THIS time it's real. All the others were dreams, but now the unthinkable is happening.

We've only ever had one fight... or one topic to fight about. Though we've fought it over and over and over, for 20 years. And it always ends the same.

I need more from him.

After the tears, the desolation, the loneliness and aching for connection, I put the walls around my heart again, and resign myself to accept what he can give me and not ask for more.

Reconnecting with a soul friend... it begins with a single email, asking for my help, after 10 years of silence, of separate lives, to protect the worlds we've chosen... and out in the ocean a wave is building.

Something's been stirring in me.

There's more for me to give. My life is about more than family and farm. The boys are in school now, we could use the extra finances... and Life is calling me to share my gifts.

But what are they?

A trip out to California. All the way from North Carolina.

Months of prayer, research, looking within. I'm wired to help people. No surprise there.

I need more training.

Counseling or Life Coaching? Never heard of Life Coaching before this. Everything in me says, YES. So I choose a training.

I've never been this far from home, and never been away from my family alone before.

Sitting on the plane, looking out over the wing, I feel God's presence there - at the very tip of the wing, as though He were perched out there looking in at me. Beckoning with a finger, for me to follow.

There in the training, overlooking the San Diego bay, with sea lions sunning themselves beside the docked sailboats,

I raise my hand. "I didn't get it right."

Everyone else is smiling, euphoric.

Seeing visions of who they are, what is unfolding in their lives.

I see myself coming home, walking through the house, and there's no place for me. I'm old, haggard, exhausted, and a shadow of myself. There's nothing of mine here, and no place to even put my suitcase.

The shell around my life cracks. I've seen what I have vowed not to see.

... the wave is building.

I cry the rest of the trip.

Is this what a baby feels like as it's being birthed?

Being pushed, compelled away from all that's been safety or comfort?

I have a body memory that reaches back to the moment of birthing. Being squeezed so hard it's crushing my face and neck. I feel fluids in my airway and no thought of breathing, just the discomfort of being born down upon. There's a weight that feels suffocating, but from pressure, not lack of air.

This feels like that.

Everything I've known, everything I've built doesn't fit me anymore. And the only way forward is crushing me.

Suffocating fear...

I have this glimpse of what could be - open expanse, wings unfurled, it catches me off guard, delighting my heart. That promise of spring... but to get there, I have to leave everything I know my life to be. My own awareness is bearing down on me like birthing contractions, refusing me a way back.

The wave is in sight.

After months of fighting - fighting with myself, fighting with my husband, fighting for a compromise that will save what we've built, the tidal wave crashes.

I move out to the studio on our farm, and he stays in the house with the boys.

The water recedes, leaving wreckage in its wake, and with it, an eerie peace.

The hives are gone.

So are the nightmares. Though in waking moments I

sometimes spin, not sure if this is yet another dream of my marriage ending, or if this time it's for real.

That shakes me.

Now I know why I cry.

And I cry all the time.

The lonely stalks me... becoming a familiar face now. The grocery store is one of the worst places. Something so innocuous reminding me that I'm no longer a wife, no longer anyone's partner. That no one has my back anymore. That the life I built is over.

I'm here alone.

Somehow, I'm not afraid of the tears anymore, or the grief.

It didn't kill me.

My life came apart, but I'm still here.

I learn how to lean into the pain now... purging wounds that have festered for decades. There's no illusion left to protect.

With that fear gone, I'm gaining strength.

I still don't like the pain. Who does?

But it's different.

I'm raw. I don't have patience for protecting illusions.

Many who were my friends avoid me.

More loss.

More tears.

And on the other side... more strength.

There's no bathroom in the studio I live in, and at 3:00am, when nature calls, I step outside under the huge night sky. That's one of the good things about living in the country. No one can see you.

Looking up, from my vulnerable position, I see Cassiopeia, Orion, and the Milky Way - the stars leaning down over me, huge and soft, like friends from outside of time. They've been here. Waiting.

A shooting star dusts the Pleiades.

Warmth rises through me, though my breath hangs in the air.

I'm not here alone.

There is a place for me.

I belong.

Something is stirring.

The question, "Is it okay for me to be?" That, which I was too scared to even ask aloud, is receiving an answer.

The answer is Yes.

I'm no longer afraid of tidal waves. I dream of the ocean still, but now when I do, I'm swimming in its depths, sometimes with heart pounding, but always with a sense of adventure.

I have a recurring vision of a huge wave now, but it doesn't bring destruction. I'm in the ocean, and it rises up from behind me with irresistible force, propelling me into my calling, into my purpose here.

… without effort, without strain.

I can let myself be held, be carried.

I can trust this. Allow myself to follow it.

I'm not alone.

I'm safe.

Like the birds navigating back to their summer breeding grounds, I too, am finding my way home.

Waking up into my life...

Elizabeth Love believes and lives the truth that our greatest gifts to others come from healing our deepest pain, and are an extension of our Essence shining to light the way. She works through Individual Coaching, Group Programs, Workshops and Retreats, and Equine Assisted Coaching, to help people create lives that are a meaningful reflection of who they are, living their purpose into the world. As a writer, she has an experiential understanding of the creative process, and a deep appreciation for the courage it takes to live authentically.

To learn more, visit www.risinginsight.com.

Or email her at Elizabeth@risinginsight.com.

Part 2

I AM Love

"When you forgive, you heal your own anger and hurt and are able to let love lead again. It's like spring cleaning for your heart."

— **Marci Shimoff**

Story Seven

Is There Perfection in Imperfection

Catherine Foster

Have you ever heard the expression, "Hit by a Mack truck?"
That expression gained new meaning to me. There came a day, an interesting day, when I jumped off a sailboat to help tie it up and landed flat on my face on a cold, wet, wood planked dock. With the movement of the boat going up and down, I was having trouble seeing where to jump and hesitated too long. The boat was nearing the dock and I had to jump before we crashed the sailboat. Everyone was yelling, "Jump. Jump off! Now!" In a split moment I built up my courage to jump. Flying through the air, time seemed to go on forever. Boom ...I landed flat on my face. My glasses went flying. My head jerked back as it hit the wood curb on the dock and I was knocked out. I lay motionless. My sister thought I was dead. My nose broken and the flesh hanging

down from the tip of my nose…. blood was everywhere, and I was in shock. I was rushed to the emergency room in a nearby town.

After that, an adventure of a new way of being in the world came together in my life.

My double vision had always been a source of feeling fractured and divided. It felt like a curse. I used to get embarrassed as one pupil would disappear off the corner of my eye and people would stare. Doctor's had me do eye exercises every day to try to strengthen the muscles. They tried thick glasses to try to get the lazy eye to stop doing what it wanted to do… disappear. As a child I just wanted to hide. I felt like a freak.

Born with strabismus, my parents did not acknowledge there was a problem until a 2nd grade teacher mentioned that my left eye would drift out of sight when I was tired. I was later told that it could have been corrected when I was a baby. Being one of seven kids, my parents were always in survival mode. I know that everything happens for a reason and that parents try their best. So I do not blame them for my eye problems.

There were years of going to the eye doctor, wearing an eye patch on the good eye to strengthen the left one and spending time in therapy. I remember as a child looking out a metal patch that had a lot of little holes. The kids at school teased me and called me Bug Eye. They were right; it did look like a bug eye. I just wanted to disappear. "Why was I different?" The experience just made me crawl more into my shyness.

My first eye operation was on my left eye when I was in 2nd grade. The hospital is a scary place as a child. My mother could not stay with me; she had the rest of the family to take care of. There I was alone in a room full of kids. They strapped me in a crib. "I'm not a baby. Why did they do that?" I remember crying myself to sleep the night before the operation. The child within felt traumatized, alone in this scary place called a hospital. I wanted to just disappear. They said that my double vision was cured from that first operation and that I would not have any more trouble for the rest of my life. Then, when I quit college at 19 to go out into the workforce, something happened. My eyes were even more challenged every day with reading and typing. I was constantly getting the most horrific headaches in the back of my head. Thinking that I needed glasses, I went back to the eye doctor. Doctors discovered that my mind was making me see as one, but my eyes were still seeing two separate images. It was as if I was always struggling with two different parts of myself trying to get my life into balance.

The surgeries continued into my early 20's. The doctor started by moving both eyes way out lengthening the eye muscles. The reality of driving and clearly seeing two images of the same car coming toward me was a shock. My mind had to acknowledge it was seeing two of everything. With each operation they would shorten muscles and tighten others slowly bringing the vision closer together. One day in my mid twenties, the doctor said he was through. My eyes were cosmetically healed. People could no longer tell that something was wrong with my eyes, but I still saw double.

If my eyes were cured, then why did I seem to break drinking glasses in the sink? Run into walls? Fall off ladders, trip going up stairs, etc.? Family and friends tagged me as clumsy. I was perpetually doomed a "Klutz."
It frustrated me that I still saw two images instead of one. Why? Was it psychological? Was I a little crazy?

Years of trying to understand my double vision has led me on an ongoing search for healing and a wonderful source to learn balance in my life. After my niece died of cancer at age 28, I became interested in studying many different healing modalities to combine with my artwork. I am an artist. I am also a Reiki Master which came out of a deep desire to not only help others, but to use on myself.

I often wonder now if vision plays a part in both our physical and spiritual lives. Am I the artist I am today because of my vision? If I did see as one, would my artwork change? My world is abstract images overlaid together weaving patterns, shapes and colors. Maybe this is why I love abstract art. Have I become the healer I am today from this search to be healed?

Painting with double vision there is no right or wrong way to create. I see crooked. No one can tell me my art is not perfect. I can't draw a straight line. But is that important to be an artist? Being reminded that my art was not perfect was something I came up against when trying to paint realism as many artists do. (Trying to paint realism was part of my search to be like everyone else. I wanted to fit in with the group, be normal). Often I would be criticized for my art not being perfect. I was painting what I saw, how could that be a bad thing? How can being who we are not be perfect?

Several times I have tried to paint exactly as I saw to help myself understand what my eyes were seeing. What was a real image and what was not was a constant question in my mind? Maybe, if I understood what I truly saw I would not bump into walls where a door was supposed to be. I started to paint still lifes and portraits, studying the double images. It was important for me to capture every line, pattern, and semblance, as one would record a story. As a painting progressed, it became harder and harder to know where to put the paintbrush. Those overlapping images kept moving around. My eyes would hurt, sting, water up. My stomach would feel sick as if I was going to throw up. My head would spin. IT WAS SO PAINFUL! Regardless, I was determined to understand what I was really seeing. I just wanted to be healed. I wanted to be seen as perfect.

What was happening in this process was that as the painting neared completion, I was not only seeing double, but as I looked at the painting I was creating, I was seeing 4 images overlapping instead of just two. Thus, I have only created 11 paintings of how I actually see. "It is what it is," I tried to tell myself. "There must be a reason that I see this way".

For a long time I wavered. Am I the healer or am I the artist? I tried to separate both of my loves, doing just the Reiki healing with clients for a few months. The deep desire to paint would build up inside me and I would spend months focusing on the art. I remember waking up in the middle of the night feeling like my heart was breaking. "Am I having a heart attack?" What gave me the most joy in life was also creating conflict in my mind, body and spirit.

92

So what is this double life really about? As an energy healer and professional artist, there is a correlation between seeing two images. I have a relationship with the spiritual world and the physical world. It is as if I have one vision in the reality of the earth and the other in the reality of the unseen. My search to be healed leads me to learning incredible energy techniques, honing skills to use to help others and expressing the healing energies into the artwork.

How did the artist and healer finally come together?

The "Mack Truck" incident changed my life! So there I was broken nose, both sides of my jaw broken, and my sinuses crushed. My neck was out of alignment. My red nose and swollen face made me look like a silly clown.

I slept on the sofa downstairs for weeks so I would not keep my husband awake at night. Just breathing was difficult and noisy. My broken jaw could not be set until the swelling went down. That was another traumatic experience, having my jaw wired shut for weeks unable to clearly speak my mind.

Was there a higher purpose to this experience? Days and nights of laying on the sofa in desperation, feeling angry with myself for being the "Klutz." I was constantly giving myself Reiki treatments, listening to healing meditations, and putting the healing tools I knew to use on myself. Finally I took my thoughts to a higher level. "OK God, I have had enough of this stuff! Falling off ladders and boats, bumping into things, accidentally breaking things. I GIVE UP! What do you want me to do? I SURRENDER!"

This may sound like a cliché, but I really did hear a booming voice say "COMBINE ART AND HEALING TOGETHER!" "Oh. Can it be that simple?" I thought. Listening to my inner voice, I followed my intuition to change my life. I stopped taking Reiki clients. Instead, the healing energy I had given to clients, I started placing into my artwork. For years it has been my desire to serve the world by using both my talents as an artist and as a healer. With intent that the highest healing energies of love, peace and joy be placed into the artwork, I pray, chant, and meditate while creating, allowing the Reiki to flow through me. It is a process of both listening to my inner vision, following my intuition and letting my hands and eyesight allow what wants to be expressed come forth. It is letting go! It is surrendering to be authentically me.

My eyes have been a huge source of healing for me in so many ways. There are still times when I get frustrated with the double vision. It continues to heal me as I embark on new ways to explore my life experience. Recently I have started doing some art just for me. Instead of putting the healing just into the artwork for others, I am using the energy to heal my deep emotions as I allow my hands to paint directly on a wood surface with juicy, colorful paints. It is a process of being in the moment with the energy surging through my body and hands. The joy is allowing my inner child to play and letting what wants to be expressed come forth, with no judgment or criticism.

I have learned through the experience with my eyes that there is perfection in imperfection! The double vision is symbolic of living my life with the awareness of seeing the physical and the unseen every day. I am truly grateful as I weave both sights into my artwork. The process is one of connecting to spirit, rising up into the consciousness of unity and truth. I do this from my heart and soul experiencing a direct connection with the world around me to serve in the highest.

I wonder, "When we heal ourselves are we also helping to heal others?" Maybe the key to living a more fulfilling and creative life is to be filled with joy being who we are. It can be as simple as accepting who we are and building on our weaknesses, which can really be our gifts.

The double vision is a gift I have been blessed with, not a curse. When I am balanced in my vision, life flows with a creative force that continually heals not only me but is my gift to the world.

Thank you God.

Catherine Foster is a professional artist, creativity coach and energy healer who uses her enthusiasm of the creative process to support and inspire others to freely express their talents in a harmonious and loving way. As a Reiki Master, Catherine combines art and healing energy together in her artwork with the intent to enliven people's homes, businesses, hospitals and medical environments. As The Creativity Whisperer, she helps empower others to live life at the fullest by clearing energy serving others to ignite their unique creativity through coaching sessions. In addition, she combines her artistic ability and the energy work with painting your essence. She is currently working on a book about creativity and how to ignite that in our daily experiences. Her big dream is to have a Sacred Creativity Retreat center for people to explore who they are creatively.

To connect with Catherine go to: www.catherinefoster.com and www.creativitywhisperer.com
  info@creativitywhisperer.com

Story Eight

Breaking the Smoked Glass
(Clear your window to see the magic of life)

Yana Mileva

"I was born in Bulgaria in a family of two teachers. My mother was putting herself and her needs always **after** everybody else's needs. My father was an alcoholic, who was putting his needs always **before** everybody else's needs. My parents wanted me to come to this world, so there I was---a fresh start for two messed up people. Needless to say, they managed to mess me up, as well---I was raised by my grandparents; I was forced into the wrong school; I was forced iton the wrong career path; I was forced out of the country. From the years living in my parent's house, I learned that I could only rely on one person---myself.

At the end of year 2011, I was at the end of my PhD studies. I was feeling unappreciated, unloved and value-less. I had been looking for a job for almost 6 months, without finding anything and my savings were quickly melting by the day. Also a few months ago a three-year long love relationship, that I expected to evolve into a marriage, had ended for me. This made me feel even more unloved, unsupported and lost. Then I was told that my work of the past four years had been, bluntly put, crap. So I was alone and jobless, and

what I had been doing in my life was deemed unworthy, which
translated into me being unworthy and useless to the world I was
living in and to the people around me."

That was what my life looked like at the end of 2011 and the dawn of the beautiful 2012 everybody was talking about as the beginning of the new era of love and human evolution. There were times when I simply couldn't breathe; times when I was choking with desperation. In the week before Christmas I just couldn't take it anymore---each moment of every day was bringing new events, words and people, who were thrusting in another dagger in my heart. And then I did the only thing I could---I stopped and breathed---it was the most difficult thing I've ever done, but it was also the only thing I could do. I breathed in and out, trying to keep myself in the present moment, because remembering the past or imagining the future was just too unbearable. When I was thinking of it all, I just couldn't believe how terrible every single thing in my life was. It was like watching a horror movie and knowing it is not and cannot be real, but it just happens to be your life! I was feeling like an observer, who was in shock and disbelief at "how is it all possibly happening?"

I had more than enough experience in self-help, healing and life coaching, so I knew the time had come for me to look into my deepest, darkest patterns, which were running my life and causing the Universe to bend the way it was bending around me. I started from the most obvious one---me feeling unappreciated and unworthy. I sat down, took in a deep breath and jumped into it. I saw an image of *the feeling of worthiness* in front of me and I asked it to unfold und reveal itself to me. What I saw was a sequence of people in my life, who have had a leading role for me (like teachers and bosses) and this sequence had at its beginning the image of my father. I had never in my life imagined that not receiving a promotion, when deserving it, or not receiving support, when needing it, could come from me not feeling loved and appreciated for my gifts by my father.

From day zero, my father had complained about how terribly I sang and how sad he was that I could not become a singer and have an easy life of singing and carrying my "instrument" everywhere with me. At first I had no idea what he was talking about---what does a three-year-old know about life struggle? Later, at age five, I was wondering if he was really serious or he was just joking. It looked too impossible that he wouldn't be able to see all the other wonderful gifts I was having---it must have been a kind of a joke from his side. Later, at age seven, I realized he was serious about it and I started rebelling against him---he was just so wrong that my life would have to be a struggle because I didn't have this unbelievably, super important talent of singing.

Unfortunately, I just couldn't tell him how wrong he was. I was constantly imagining fictitious dialogs with him and was spending hours crafting my arguments, but never actually dared to speak up. He never accepted another opinion and always saw his own as the ultimate truth. And he was like that when he was sober. When he was drunk, which happened to be most of the evenings, I simply had to stay in my room and hide from his temper, too scared to even go out to use the bathroom, make some noise and be noticed. I was scared, but my father, the most important man in my life, couldn't protect me, for he was the thing I needed protection from. I was scared, but my mother, the most important woman in my life, couldn't protect me, for she herself was too scared to even protect herself. And I did the only thing I could---grew strong on the inside and was always ready to protect and save myself, without expecting external support. I knew my own value; I knew I was strong; I knew I was capable. So, imagine my constant confusion, when knowing I was so strong with so many gifts, I kept on being faced all throughout my life by people, who didn't think me worthy and who were not appreciating me for who I was. And oh boy, did I spend years in the company of each one of those people! So there I was, at the end of 2011 and the dawn of the beautiful 2012, facing yet another person, who was seeing me and my work as worthless and pure crap. I want to say that I got angry, shouted the truth in his face, gave him a wake-up slap and went on with my life. But I didn't. All I could do was breathe and even that was hard, as my chest was tight and each breath was choking me.

Christmas 2011 came and I got the chance to run away from my life and go back to the fairy-tale of my childhood in the house of my grandparents. There I wasn't feeling the choking tightness in my chest; there I could take a step back and see the picture from a distance. That is when I saw this pattern of lack of appreciation running throughout my entire life. I was petrified. I was petrified of what it had caused in my life, but even more of what it could cause. And there I stood, a grown up woman, equipped with all of my self-healing knowledge and experience, needing to heal my sweet, dear, five-year-old self, who was still feeling scared to go to the bathroom.

Some time ago I had watched a presentation online, where the person invited the audience members to rewrite their life-story the way they wanted it to have happened. I stopped and I thought. What did I want my life to look like? I wanted people to love me beyond anything imaginable. I wanted to be successful. I wanted to be doing something that was meaningful, and that I was passionate about. I wanted to be living with a supportive and compassionate man, who was madly in love with me and whom I madly loved. I wanted to wake up in the morning eager to be awake and to welcome my day, the people I was going to meet and the things I was going to do. That is what I wanted my life to look like. And I went back to the drawing board. I knew what I wanted; I just didn't know the path to it. I decided that I had been trying for too long to save my life and myself and I had failed. My life was way heavier on my heart than I could bear or deal with. And at this moment something in me died. The struggle, the grasping for knowing the solution, the desire to be in control of life---all died. I gave up struggling and trying too hard to fix things in my life. I gave up being the strong one, the brave one. I had tried too many times to be that and I had failed. We all read many books throughout our life, hear many speeches and meet a lot of people. Most of the things we forget. Some of them stick around though and hide until it is time for them to surface. That is what happened to me---I remembered what I read once in a book: "Let go and let God." I decided that I couldn't do anything else. I cannot force people to hire me. I cannot force people to like me. I cannot force a man to love me. I decided to give up and let God rearrange things for me. The Universe has its ways---you will pass by a magazine stand and glimpse at the title of a newspaper, check its website out of curiosity and a month later you find yourself working your dream job at this newspaper; you drop your groceries in the food store and a man helps you collect them---a year later you two are happily married together. We cannot force the Universe to bend. We cannot force synchronicities to happen. So, I decided to give up trying and to let the Universe bend itself and present to me all the wonderful coincidences it is capable of. When I had my moments of doubt, I imagined the Earth, "hanging" in the void of the cosmos, and I chuckled at my doubt that the force that had created a huge "hanging" planet could not create a job for me. And on top of that I already had a proof that the Universe can indeed arrange the right things to happen at the right moment---I had experienced it before.

Three years ago I wanted to expand my abundance level. I was looking into what money and relationship patterns have been running my life (the relationship with money is also a relationship). I discovered and cleared some "fascinating" things about myself and the unconscious programs that had been running my life. One day, while browsing a famous social-network site, I stumbled across a video---it was a video of people dancing and having fun, but the weird thing about it was that they were all at the gym. The title of the video was "Zumba Fitness®". I had never ever heard of Zumba® before in my life. I googled it, found its official website and searched for classes in my neighborhood.

Zumba® is a Latin-flavored fitness-dance program that uses rhythms from all around the world. I love dancing and this thing looked like so much fun! Unfortunately, there were no classes within 25 miles distance of where I lived. Then a funny thought crossed my mind: "If there are no classes, maybe I can offer one?" I opened the official Zumba® website again and looked for instructor workshops---it turned out there was a workshop scheduled on the date I had already booked tickets to London to visit a friend of mine and the venue was within 10 minutes walking-distance from my friend's house! Between the moment I spotted that Zumba® video on the social network site and the moment I hit "Register", only 15 minutes in total had passed. And just like that---I became a Zumba® instructor. Nowadays, I teach classes of up to 300 people; newspaper and magazine journalists have been writing articles about my Zumba® classes; TV stations have come to film us. And needless to say, I have dramatically increased my abundance level. Just like that. Just within 15 minutes.

So I knew that the Universe can provide and I knew that having my intention out there and clearing my emotional baggage around it was all it took for the Universe to deliver my synchronicities. I decided to rewrite my story.

"I was born in Bulgaria in the family of two beautiful people. Both of my parents were teachers. My mother was a loving person, who was always ready to help and support a child in need. My father was a cheerful person, who loved life and was full of creative artistic ideas. Both of my parents created me in love and wanted me to come to this world. So there I was---a fresh start to two full of life and hope young people. My parents were still students, when they brought me to this world and I spent my first years in the loving, caring presence of my grandparents. My parents wanted the best for me and as math teachers they believed that math carries the knowledge of the entire Universe within itself (and they were right). I graduated with flying colors from a math high school as well as from my undergraduate studies. I had the chance to live abroad, where I met a star-cloud of wonderful people, coming from all different countries and cultures and I found out that no matter skin color, background, religion or gender, people can always be your most dear friends.

At the end of 2011, I was graduating from a PhD program and had discovered several of my greatest gifts and passions. I was looking for my 'next thing to do' and in the beginning I didn't know what that was. Every time something was crossing my path, I was asking my heart if that was what I was looking for, but my heart kept on telling me to keep on searching. My being was vibrating with the excitement of finding that wonderful aligned 'thing' and was ready to wait for it for as long as it takes. My heart was smiling every time I was thinking that ending a three-year-long unhappy relationship finally gave me the chance to find the man I longed for. I was surrounded by friends and dear ones, who loved me deeply; I knew what I wanted from life and I had the chance to create and completely reshape my life from scratch. The Universe was giving me the space to recreate every aspect of my life the way my heart was craving it to be."

Both of those stories are true. The first story is written by my five-year old self, who was running my life, from a space of fear and sadness. The second story is written by my higher self, who realizes that we all have our path and our lessons to learn, who does not blame and who is here to create from a space of love. Both stories are valid. I just chose to live my life from the place of the second story. By choosing the second story, I not only moved into a space of creation and expansion, but also realized how blind I was for the actual reality. I realized I was still seeing my parents as the people I knew thirty years ago. They have changed tremendously. My mother grew strong and independent. My father stopped drinking more than fifteen years ago.

Rewriting my story, rewrote not only my life, but also the relationship with my parents. My heart swells with love, appreciation and respect, realizing how hard it must have been for my mom to face her fears and to stand up for herself and how strong my dad must have been to fight his addiction out of the love for his child and his wife. The gift of healing this relationship is the biggest gift I could have ever given to myself.

A month after I rewrote my life story, what I was looking for appeared magically on my path. In the last week of my studies, I got the phone call for that dream job. A month later I moved to a new city, met new people and made new friends. I was no longer jobless, unappreciated and lost. And, oh, that dream guy... he's also in the making☺. Was I surprised by all the synchronicities that had occurred? Not really. Was I happy? You bet! People have been reporting weird outbursts of jumping and dancing activities in my home. I have no idea what they are talking about☺.

It is sometimes hard to face your reality, but it is always worth the courage to rewrite it.

Yana Mileva: *"I have stepped on the road of self-discovery many, many years ago. Since I remembered myself, the questions of the universe have been occupying a major part of my thoughts. I remember reading a book about the great pyramids, as a child, and wondering who was the one who built them and who are we---those wonderful, mysterious Earthlings, who can't build them now (or so we think). My questions refined with time and I stopped asking, "where did the stars come from," but "where did the soul come from," "what is time" and "why do people face suffering." In this holographic universe, where each part is contained in each other, we all have the freedom to focus on the part, which excites us the most and then we automatically understand the rest of it all, as well. By delving into the realms of human soul and energy field, I found the answers to my old "pyramid and stars" questions, too. Now I have others :).*

http://www.joyridecoaching.com"

Story Nine

Gift of Love

Brenda Jacobi

Peering out the window in search of the first star, I still remember being deeply engaged in conversation with God and The Universe as I entertained myself on that 10-hour drive across the desert to grandma's house. I was 8 years old and I decided that there was no time like the present, to take action on what I wanted most, to KNOW TRUE LOVE. "Star light, star bright, first star I see tonight, I wish I may, I wish I might, have the wish, I wish tonight…."

And with those words, I felt complete. Could it be that easy? I was envisioning being happily married to the man of my dreams whom I deeply adored who equally cherished and honored me. Together we would birth the family of our dreams wanting for nothing traveling the world and having fun!

Summer Olympics of 1976, Nadia Comaneci scored her 4 perfect 10's in women's gymnastics, history in the making being captured on live television right in front of me. I was 10, and in that moment, I knew I had to become a gymnast!

While I loved gymnastics and being in the gym I hated competition! Watching Nadia was sheer beauty! Competition was anything but…. Competitive gymnastics felt as though I were judging my very soul! You want for too much. You settle for too little. Would the real Brenda please stand up? Why can't I just be me?

Only who was I, the *real* Brenda? Beauty? Or Beast? All I knew was that the closer I got to the soul of the gymnastics the more frightened and chicken I became. My body inadvertently disengaged should I start to shine. I was dumbfounded though relieved to be safe. I was terrified at being good at anything except being nice and getting good grades.

Inwardly, I justified my behavior by telling myself that others needed to win more than I did. That way, they would have the opportunity to know that God loved them as much as I knew HE loved me. My fear of chastisement from a God who loves me, lessened as well.

The idea of heaven on earth seemed an open invitation for a game of Chess between God and the devil with me as pawn. Would God try me as HE did HIS faithful servant Job? Could I endure such brutal anguish and still sing God's praises? How far would God allow the devil to go with me? Would I still be able to walk? Would I even want to know myself? I wasn't open to finding out. It was up to me to keep myself safe.

My beam of life was straight and narrow. Don't fly too high or falter too low on the bars of life. Remain parallel to the will of God and live. Please God, no vaulting! I may splat and never get up!

I scored my perfect 10's on the home front. I was *expert* at avoiding the wrath of my father. I nailed it every time! It helped to be quiet and make no waves. He practiced *tough love* and he made no apologies for it. "Spank first, ask, questions later". Later never came.

Obedience, humility, acceptance, and indulgences (for the souls of poor sinners) was the path to heaven. Unless, God had other plans for you, HE seemed to like making exceptions: The Blessed Virgin Mary, Joseph, her celibate spouse and Jesus, who died on the cross. Would I recognize God's special request of me or would I fear it as the devil deceiving me?

The more vibrant, powerful and beautiful I felt the closer I could feel the impending wrath of God upon me. Appeasing God was a full time job. Thank God Nadia was Romanian! My father said that religion was against the law in her country. Lucky her! She needn't fear God for being SO BEAUTIFUL!

Why can't I have the freedom to love like that? Is my heart really so evil (even though it is fashioned in the image and likeness of God) that I cannot be trusted to discern for myself what is good or evil? Must I really be damned to hell for daring to be in opposition to God or the Pope?

The power to love openly and honestly because you want to! TRUE FREEDOM! SHEER BLISS!

Why are there two types of marriage in my church? Aren't they both to God? Why can't I serve The Church and be married to a human? Aren't they both equally in service to God and The Church without one or the other being of a higher spiritual calling? Yet, I have been led to believe that marriage to a human is more geared toward those of us who lack self-control. Self-control? How is my desire to share myself with a fellow human being and birth a child lacking self-control? Or does it have to do with purity? Isn't one as pure as the other? AHHHHH!

By 15, I stopped competing in gymnastics in the hopes of relinquishing such ambiguity from my life. I went solely into coaching. I could remain part of the gym, sport and people that I loved ever hopeful that God would remember my one request and find me selfless enough to allow me to have it. There was a new lift to my aerials and my Russian split leaps, were to die for!

That's about the time our gym got a new head team coach. I was ever curious straining my ears for details of him. I didn't dare ask! That wasn't my way. I watched. I listened. I learned. All the while asking God, "Is he the one?" Is he the one my heart has longed for and that I have prayed for all these years?

Could a girl like me, from a tumbleweed town in the desert, a gymnast, who was too afraid to win, be so lucky? I supposed that only time would tell. And how it did.... I was naturally drawn to him. He was older and seemingly unattached with discerning tastes. The team kids flocked to him and people were genuinely happy. Would I trust him to spot me on a double back? Would he be willing? (YES! I still smile!)

I wanted to know everything about him. Hmmm, I wondered if that made me selfish again? I turned to God the only way I knew how. God, I trust in YOUR Divine Timing. I place my heart in YOUR hands. Mold me, as YOU will. I will just be love.

It Happened One Summer, (song by, The Motels) Summer of "83", I was 17 now and going into my senior year of high school. I was invited to hang out for a hot summer's night swim. I was told that *he*, my gem of the gym, (the head team coach) would be there and did I want to go? *Did I want to go?* Are you kidding me? YES! I just went. No hesitation. No stopping to count the costs. We never swam that night. He kissed me! I kissed back! God was it delicious!!!

After that night, I held his gaze as he equally held mine. I couldn't help myself. My eyes just flew to him; I caught myself wondering if I was allowed? Could I be so privileged? Did I need permission? Should I not stop, someone would notice and then what? My eyes sought him out wherever either of us went. When he wasn't in the gym my eyes paced for him not settling until they rested upon him.

And as we became more intimate and engaged in our interactions, ever curious and concerned for the safety of my soul, I needed to know, is this love or is it lust? Did there have to be a difference? The Church said there was and so, I had no choice but to follow suit. Damn! I wanted both! It must have something to do with Robert Palmer's song Addicted to Love. Everything was happening so fast. Maybe I was addicted? I felt so great! I couldn't get enough of him, this! My father was an alcoholic as was my grandfather... Shit! Addiction runs in both sides of my family! Worse than that, I almost don't care! I never felt so fearless! Would this be the death of me?

When I looked into his eyes, I saw Jesus. I could never decide if his eyes were brown, hazel or amber... All I knew was, they were golden, like his heart! He wasn't Catholic or of any creed and while I didn't care, I knew my father would...

What to do??? Perfect? No. Unblemished? YES! Prideful and stubborn, YES, but, I liked that! He spoke his mind! He spoke his heart! BEAUTIFUL!

He smoked though never around me. He was always fresh and clean. He had tattoos and the saunter of a sailor.

I could count on him. He and gymnastics made sense. They were logical and ordered. Their magic was palpable! Seen by the naked eye! MYSTICAL! The mysteries of my faith were just that, mysterious...

"Lord, I am not worthy to receive YOU but, only say the word and I shall be healed." "Of what?" I wondered? I spoke that statement week after week before receiving the Eucharist. I *cringed* every time. Now, God, if you would be so kind, there's this guy...

He seems to cherish me though I have no idea why?

God? Did you Send Me An Angel (Song by Real Life) or are you testing me? Affection wanted to burst out of me in leaps and bounds (a first) could I dare...   (My family doesn't touch.)

Lucky Star by, Madonna, that's exactly how I felt, the LUCKIEST of ALL! He stood up for, and to me. Sometimes, maddening yet, how I wished I could do that! He awakened a beast within me, Hungry Like the Wolf by Duran Duran. Is this the kind of love that becomes tainted and spoiled leaving people broken, tattered and in ruins? Does passion rival love for you God?

My back no longer hurt when I once thought it would break in two! I felt energized and like a million bucks though neither of us had much money. I rose with the morning light. I felt like a queen though he never "officially" asked me out. He made it clear that he would never shame or humiliate my dignity. What I wondered was, would he be willing to admit to me in public what he acknowledged to me in private?

Was there a reason besides my age that few knew of "us"? We are an "us" aren't we? Clearly, we had fallen in love! It was obvious, wasn't it? He seemed to be waiting for something but, what?

He wanted to coach an Olympian. I wanted to own my own gym. How could I tell him? I could bare my chest to him but not like this! Heart, These Dreams, would God dangle our dreams just beyond our reach as a means of purifying our hearts? A cross I could never bear!

Alone again, at last! No need for words now.

Our hearts, how they beat as one, intrinsic, instinctual, as if on cue… Their rapid beats matching that of our breaths, braided, intertwined, rhythmic as though married into one…

I was captivated! Mesmerized! How easily I followed his lead…   How naturally he followed mine….   His words, how they dripped like honey, off his tongue, drizzling down my neck, traveling down my chest and landing, like a perfect ten right in my heart, never to depart.

My heart how it danced and leaped spiraling and radiating upward and outward exploding into a STAR, across a night of LIGHT, FILLED SKY! Is this the Milky Way, the Big Dipper and yet, "I", "WE", a mere spark?

Did I die and go to Heaven and through only a kiss? And yet, what a kiss! Should I never know another, I've lived a lifetime in just this ONE. Yet, I'm still here upon the Earth? (A question too big to ask.)

Can I remain forever? Can we? Though I see you not, I feel you, everywhere.

Yet, where am I? And how did I get here when last I knew, I was in the arms of my lover? Ahhh, YES, snuggled in the arms of my lover safe and warm on the mush mat in the darkened gym, filled only by the light of the street filtering in through the dusty windows of the night sky.

Where you begin or I end, is no more. We are ONE and yet NOT joined… *Bone of my bone, flesh of my flesh*… Were the words that flashed before my mind as if spoken to me by an unfamiliar voice from deep within me? I knew their origin but not their source. This translation seemed foreign, out of context. It felt literal, alive and visceral within me where as I had always been taught to deny *the flesh*. Seek the spiritual integrity. What does this mean??? Nobody ever said anything about this! Body, mind and spirit in ONE! He is not Adam and I, not Eve. When he took my hand, it fit like a glove!

God, "Try as I might, I have never loved YOU like this!" I have no shame. I have no fear.

Until….   After….   He spoke those three precious

words, "I love you."

That tumbled right out of his mouth and rolled off of his tongue.

And while I knew what he meant, I didn't know what this would mean...

Does he "do" marriage just as I want? After my stupor of silence, determining that I needed more time to discover his intent for fear that I would push him away; because all I wanted to say was, "If you mean always and forever, "I love you."

And not knowing what to do and knowing that I needed to do something, I spoke a lie though true. "I like you.... A lot!"

And, No, while we never did have sex that night or any other, we never stopped making love. Berlin's song, Sex, I'm a.... played hourly on the radio seemingly to beg me to answer the question, who am I? A song that I secretly loved though thought I must hate! One night with him could never have been enough. I wanted all of him for myself in marriage or nothing at all.

Seeking to clear the air and not knowing how, I turned and walked away. There was no greater sacrifice that I could think to make. And with the words of Quarterflash, Harden My Heart, I did just that. Our gym disbanded and we went our separate ways, on the journey of life...

All the while keeping my transgression of love buried deep in my heart. Safe where not even God could destroy it.

I did my best to move on afraid to confide in anyone. I moved out of state and married a fellow Catholic, believing we held God and love in common. We rarely spoke of either. Prayer and God seemed banned from our house though we went to church routinely. He built his dream career. I birthed our children, five daughters and a son.

Our son was born only after my awakening. Awakening into the realization that my experience of love was just that, Eros love. God's love for me, my love for God, this man's love for me and my love for him. I never knew that God could possess a soul the way I was taught the devil could. I finally discovered that what I feared (might be evil) was God! God alive and well within me! He loves me that much! He loves YOU that much!

The only permission I ever needed was my own. The conviction was always in my heart. God never gave up on me. He gave me all the time I needed. All the time in the world...

Hi, I'm **Brenda Jacobi**, *Essence Coach*

I reside in Portland, Oregon where I am continuously growing and expanding my ability to love and be in JOY in my LIFE. While I no longer fear for the state of my soul (or that of others) I do find it humorous to recall how truly frightened I once was. I thoroughly ENJOY the certainty of Universal Law while I more easily embrace change as a norm in life. Being human is so much easier NOW! Coaching to YIELD THE FRUIT OF YOUR DESIRE is **MY PASSION***!*

Why be in FEAR when you can be in **LOVE***?*

www.BrendaJacobi.com
Brenda@EssenceCoaches.com

Story Ten

A Spy in the House of Art

Lisa Morningstar

There was a time when I thought it would be fun to live the bohemian writer lifestyle as Henry Miller did in the 1930's—meeting with all the writers and artists of the day in cafes, having mind blowing conversations and exchanges of meaning. For me it all began in the summer of '79, in Berkeley CA, on Telegraph Ave, inside The Mediterranean Café— known as the Med by the locals. The Med is a two-story café with high ceilings. The upstairs is a loft overlooking all the patrons below and the action outside on the street. I had been devouring Henry Miller's books, *Tropic of Cancer, Black Spring* and *Tropic of Capricorn* that chronicled his lives and loves as an expatriate in Paris. His writings portrayed a stream of consciousness and a lust for life, to such a degree that his books were banned in the United States. I resonated with and was delighted by his cutting edge rebellion and creativity.

The avant-garde writers and creative artists hung out at these Paris cafes exchanging passionate ideas with each other. They were the Bohemians.

While in Paris, Miller befriended a woman writer, Anaïs Nin, who also became his lover and critic. She documented their relationship in her diaries. I read most of them. Her diaries were brought to life in the 1992 feature film, *Henry and June*. I adopted her writing style in my own work. I resonated so much with the title of Nin's novel, *A Spy in the House of Love*, that I named my own writings *A Spy in the House of Art*. That new title seemed to fit me for two reasons: One reason being that *"the spy in my head"* was insatiably curious about the diverse ethnicities, backgrounds and realities of my quirky new California friends who were radically different than the people I grew up with in New York, and the other reason being that since childhood I'd self-identified as an artist and that gave me license to adopt certain attributes that I perceived came with being an artist, such as creating my own rules how to go about living and not being good in math.

Years later I'd refine those thoughts and simply say that I've always looked at life through the lens of an artist. What I mean by that is that there is more to life than just what simply lays in front of you - there are the symbols and metaphors and colors and layers, each one having their individual interpretations that weave and patch together like a quilt to form the big picture. I wasn't taught to think along those concepts; it just evolved quite naturally, allowing me to play with my creativity in a way that was fun and different from the standard way of thinking.

That summer I was so taken by reading about the Bohemian café culture in Paris of the 1930's that I created my own Bohemia right there, upstairs at the Med. I set the stage in my head and transformed myself into one of the writers that Henry Miller and Anaïs Nin wrote about in their books. I went by the name Samantha. I told everyone that I was writing a book, but I really wasn't in the traditional sense. I was actually writing stories about all the diverse people that I surrounded myself with and the connections, 'synchronicities,' that I saw with my relationship to them. My friend Cecilia was my rendition of Anaïs Nin. She was an exotic, European beauty who wore colorful harem pants and velvet ballet slippers. We'd sit at my table and plot our Lucy and Ethel style schemes together. Our schemes were mischievous and elaborate, yet we carried them out with ease and grace (which is code for we never got caught).

Being the Introverted Extrovert, I had two spots in the café that I hung out at. For privacy, the best place to sit was upstairs, way in the back, at the table by the fan. Then I could write and observe the action but not participate in it. Very few people sat back there so it was a nice and quiet space to write and draw. In contrast, for social interaction I'd hold court at one of the tables upstairs by the railing. From there I could also see my friends and wave to them if they entered the café. Miller's days in Paris found him in the company of many characters and that was the same with me. The Med was my office. I'd ask the writers, the artists, the activists, the foreigners and yes, even the crazies, questions about their lives and then listen to their stories and then write about them later. On Saturdays, the view from my table was the artists working their craft booths out on the avenue. Occasionally the classic Berkeley eccentric walked by, like Julia the poet, who we called the "bubble lady" because she blew out a stream of bubbles from her wand when she walked down Telegraph Ave. The different ways that people express their creativity has always been of great interest to me.

In the late 1970's there were only a few resources available for seeking out information about my strange, inherent interests. To my family, and even to myself, terms like "fortune telling" or "occult" suggested that other realities, outside of the everyday, familiarities actually existed and parts of me truly wanted to belief that, did believe that, and also ashamed of believing that. To me, it was so much more than fortune telling. Astrology, numerology and tarot were my back door into self-healing. The fact that the planets stood for personality traits and that the numbers told your life path and the pictures on the tarot cards symbolized a story inspired and excited me to know that there were other ways to decipher the meaning of things. On one hand you could argue that venturing into these realms was a welcome escape from where I came but what I sought out was not about the escape, it was about trying to solve myself however non-traditional the method was. Looking back I'd say that the seeds of my inquiry into self-exploration and intuition were planted that summer.

Across the street from the Med was Shambhala Booksellers; they sold "new age" books and the classics of spiritual and esoteric literature. Once inside the store, I'd get both over stimulated and overwhelmed and I didn't know whether it was from the burning incense or the browsing over the Carlos Castaneda series or the tarot cards or the numerology books or a combination of them all. Haven't you ever experienced being inside a bookstore when a book practically jumps off the shelf into your arms and if by magic opens up to the pages that you were meant to read?

Back at the Med, there were a stream of oddly, leering characters who visited me at my table to talk about wizardry or the occult and some even asked me if I wanted to go somewhere with them to get a "healing," which confused me even more because I knew that I wasn't "sick." And then there was my friend, a street vendor who read Tarot cards for a donation on Telegraph Ave. who eventually went crazy and blinded himself.

Fast forward 30 years and now you can easily find a plethora of information about intuition and synchronicity and spirituality online and in stores, written by ordinary people like you and me. Back then developing your consciousness was just for gurus and holy people. It was during those early Berkeley years that unbeknownst to me, the seeds were being planted in my unconscious awareness that I was destined to create a business based around the concepts of intuition, energy and synchronicity when I was in my mature years. Those interests have ripened into the same skill set that I use to read energy as an Intuition Coach.

Looking back I can also say that Henry Miller was an early mentor even though I didn't work with him personally. Had it been possible, I would have time- travelled back to that era to have those experiences he wrote about. His books inspired me to imitate his Bohemian lifestyle, to write, to meet with interesting, creative people, and to live a café lifestyle, as I perceived artists to live. We had some things in common. Both of us had Brooklyn roots. We both identified as rebels. His books extolled a freedom that was too racy for the time so he exiled himself to Paris to have the freedom he craved in order to express himself. I never saw the value of fitting in with the status quo. After high school my peers and I took different paths. They went to colleges in upstate New York and I took my $300 savings and moved across the country to California. Subconsciously I must have thought that if I moved far enough from my family and friends and everything familiar, then my disconnected parts would be left behind too, but of course they weren't.

Back then I probably would have agreed that I was a "seeker" however I didn't exactly know yet what I was seeking – that would come to me much later on, as this story illustrates the initial toe-dipping stages of my journey into awakening and the puzzle pieces didn't quite fit together yet. I inherently understood the language of symbols and metaphor and knew – but didn't know how I knew - that inner and outer coincidences appeared in patterns, that it was important to be on the lookout for clues, and when you followed those clues, similar to following the bread crumbs in the Hansel and Gretel story, that they would lead you to a place where an opportunity would present itself or you would get an answer letting you know that you were on the right track.

I invite you to follow the bread crumbs in your own life and then notice what unfolds for you and what form it comes in.

Lisa Morningstar *met her husband-to-be on a blind date not too long after her Bohemian summer experience at the Med. At first glance, she noticed his eyes twinkling behind his John Lennon glasses and the lyrics of Linda Ronstadt's song, Just One Look played loudly in her head. She followed the "breadcrumb" and it led them both to long-lasting love. Together with her husband, they are business owners and live in the San Francisco Bay Area. Lisa enjoys walking in nature, visiting wineries, and attending outdoor concerts and farmer's markets.*

Lisa helps public speakers embody their personal power so that when they speak, the audience feels the confidence, the warmth and the expertise of the speaker's message and is naturally drawn into the offer.

In her intuitive coaching practice, Lisa helps her clients unravel and heal the resistant behaviors that stand in the way of shining in the spotlight.

*Visit Lisa's website at **www.leadbyintution.com** to book a discovery session to talk about the right support and package for you.*

Story Eleven

Glastonbury: The Heart Chakra of the Planet

Kathleen Nelson Troyer

My fascination with Glastonbury, England began when I was in college and read The Mists of Avalon by Marion Zimmer Bradley. The book is set in the legendary land of Avalon, near Glastonbury. It is the tale of King Arthur told through the eyes of his sister, the priestess Morgaine. This wonderful work of historical fiction opened up a whole new world to me. I felt so intrigued with the world she described in the book, the ancient goddess religions that honored our earth, the divine feminine and the healing arts all woven in with the tale of King Arthur. I knew that I had to go to Glastonbury someday. I didn't have to wait long for my dream to come true. The following summer, I had the opportunity to travel abroad. My aunt was planning a trip to Rosslyn, Scotland, where my paternal grandfather was from, and she invited me to join her. Before meeting my Auntie Helen in Edinburgh, I went to Glastonbury. I remember how excited I felt on the long bus ride. As the bus approached Glastonbury the green hills became even greener and my heart skipped a beat as I saw the great hill, The Glastonbury Tor. As soon as I arrived, I felt like I was home. It was magical. The rolling green hills were enchanting as I hiked up to the Tor. I fell in love with the gardens at The Chalice Well. I sat in the gardens for hours listening to the gentle sound of running water and feeling the sunshine soak into my body. I felt my heart open while watching the sacred waters come out of the mouth of the Lion's Head fountain. The scenery was very much like it was described in The Mists of Avalon.

One afternoon I was doing some shopping on High Street and I stumbled into a metaphysical bookstore, Pandora's Box. As I was browsing in the store, the owner Jim introduced himself to me and we chatted about all sorts of things from crop circles to crystals. Jim seemed to be an expert on the ancient stone circles of Stonehenge and Avebury. Both of these stone circles are within an hour's drive of Glastonbury. Jim explained to me that the two circles each represented the divine masculine and feminine. Stonehenge was the more masculine of the two stone circles and Avebury carries the energy of the divine feminine.

The afternoon wouldn't have been complete without talking about The Mists of Avalon, and the local Arthurian lore for which Glastonbury was famous. I learned that people come from all over the world to visit Glastonbury, and for many, it was like a spiritual pilgrimage. People seem to be called there in a similar way that folks are called to other sacred sites like Jerusalem, Mecca and Fatima. Jim explained to me that Glastonbury sits on ancient ley lines that are power vortexes on the planet. There are at least two major ley lines that connect on the top of the hill at the Glastonbury Tor. He also told me that Glastonbury is the heart chakra of planet earth. Our conversation left me feeling even more drawn to and connected with the place.

Before I knew it the entire afternoon had passed. As we parted, Jim told me that he had a gift for me. He gave me a button type pin that said: YOUR APPROVAL IS NOT ESSENTIAL. **He** told me that this was an important lesson for me. He encouraged me to care less about other people's opinions of me. As we parted ways, he told me that it was important to trust my intuition and when in doubt, to follow my heart.

☼♥☼♥☼♥☼♥☼♥☼♥☼♥☼♥

I was a surprise baby for my family. My mother was 34 with an 11-year-old daughter and a 9-year-old son. My father was in his early 40's and a merchant marine by trade; he was at sea more than he was at home. My sense is, although my parents loved me dearly, that my arrival was not a pleasant surprise. It wasn't until recently that I became aware that there is a part of me that has apologized for my existence. I never quite felt like I fit into the family. I was a challenge from the get go. I was told that I was "too sensitive" and "wanted too much." I had to fight to have my needs heard. And then I was told that I was "too angry." My mother was a practicing alcoholic until she found Alcoholics Anonymous and became sober when I was eight. Pre-AA was somewhat chaotic and post AA involved tagging along with Mom to countless speakers meetings and AA holiday potlucks. I knew what "skid row" and "hitting bottom" were before my 9th birthday. At the time I didn't love being dragged to the meetings with Mom, but now I feel grateful for being exposed to the healing and transformation that unfolded there.

In retrospect, being the youngest of the three kids was a blessing, but growing up in that environment had its challenges. My older brother had unresolved anger issues; and I took the brunt of them. He behaved like a bully and dished out regular emotional abuse to me. His focus was on my being overweight. It was a challenging environment to develop a healthy self-esteem. By the time I was ten or so, it became clear to me that our home was not like other homes. While most of my friends felt safe in their homes, I did not. Our family had lots of unresolved feelings and unmet needs that seemed to manifest in anger, frustration, sarcasm and depression. It was not an environment where authentic self-expression was encouraged. I knew from a pretty young age that I wanted a different life for myself.

I was the first one in our family to go to college and to travel abroad. That brought up mixed emotions and responses from my family. On one level they were happy for me and proud of my accomplishments and on another level they resented me for pushing hard to break out of the family culture and norms. And yet, I still craved their love and approval. It was a complex dynamic and I am grateful to have had some amazing women outside of my family to support, mentor and show me that I could make different choices. That support was essential to my growth and aspirations for a better life.

When Jim in Glastonbury gave me that button that said, "Your approval is not essential," it hit me at the core of my being. This man that I had just met reached deep into my soul and gave me a touchstone that would serve me for the rest of my life. That afternoon with Jim in Glastonbury turned out to be a highlight of my travels. I cherished the pin he gave me for many years. I shared it with my girlfriends when they needed a reminder about "the approval of others." It was passed from friend to friend and eventually made its way to others. I am not sure where it ended up. Even though I don't have physical possession of the pin, the richness of the learning will be with me always. I learned that I wasn't the only one who longed for approval and belonging. As women, we are taught to be good little girls from the beginning of our lives and to seek approval from others. Many of us have built our lives around fitting in and seeking approval. Twenty years later, after much therapy, coaching and spiritual exploration, there are still times when I need to remind myself of Jim and his pin.

When I returned home from my summer trip, I began my last year of college and immediately started planning my next trip back to Glastonbury. I was also offered a part time job in a store called Red Rose Gallery in the Marina district of San Francisco. The company's slogan was "products to empower people." The store had an elegant atmosphere and great products; a nice combination of books, crystals, jewelry and divination tools like tarot cards and runes. It was a fun place to work and I loved working there. I met some wonderful people at Red Rose, some of whom are still in my life twenty years later.

My co-worker Ronna and I became fast friends. She taught me how to develop my intuition and my spiritual self. Ronna was in her early 30's at the time and became very much like an older sister and mentor to me. We often worked the closing shift at the store together and on slower evenings she shared some of her tools with me. She taught me how to ground, center, and connect to the earth with a grounding cord. She also showed me how to connect with something she called a "healing cord" which was a column of light above my head that connects us with God, or universal source energy and draws a stream of gold down through our bodies. She taught me to create an energetic bubble around myself for protection and to pull my energy back from other people and to send other people's energy back to them. She also shared information about our body's energy and chakra system.

Ronna had read a book that we carried in the store by Sondra Ray, entitled **Inner Communion**. She felt very aligned with the book, especially the introduction by Robert Coon. The name sounded familiar to me because Jim, from Glastonbury, had talked about Robert's work. Robert was an American living in Glastonbury and in 1967 he downloaded the planetary chakra system that can be found at *www.earthchakras.org*. Ronna became intrigued by Robert's work and started doing some research of her own. About a week or two before my departure date for my graduation trip, she decided to join me on the Glastonbury leg of my trip. I was delighted and excited to be going on a spiritual pilgrimage to Glastonbury with Ronna who had become a dear friend, spiritual mentor and teacher to me. I was very excited to share my special place with her.

We arrived at London Heathrow airport in the late afternoon and stayed the first night in London. We ate dinner at an Indian restaurant and went to sleep early. At the time there was only one bus per day to Glastonbury. We had planned to take the five o'clock bus the following afternoon; however we woke up at the crack of dawn hearing a crow's calling. Both of us were excited to get to Glastonbury and didn't want to wait all day for the bus. So, we decided to hitchhike, and it was an adventure! We spent the bulk of the day making our way to Glastonbury. Several folks took us part of the way and we arrived in town right before five.

The first thing we did was go to Pandora's Box to see Jim and his wife Sue, but the store was closed. On the door was a flyer for a workshop on Robert's planetary chakra system that started at six. We grabbed a quick bite to eat and headed over to the address on the flyer, which was about a half a block up High Street. It turned out that Ronna and I were the only two participants for the workshop that night and we got to have a private session with Kevin, the workshop leader.

What I remember most about the workshop was Kevin arranging for us to meet Robert Coon for lunch the following day. Robert discussed his healing work with sacred sites and his planetary chakra system as well as his college days in San Francisco. Ronna shared our story of meeting at Red Rose Gallery the previous fall and discovering Robert's work through Sondra Ray's book and our story of being called to leave earlier than the bus, Robert nodded and grinned and said that it sounded like we were travelling along the magical currents.

We were fortunate to spend more time with Robert on that trip. On one occasion we were hiking in an area called "The Glastonbury Zodiac" and in the woods I felt the presence of fairies. I couldn't see them but felt their playful energy encouraging me to laugh more and not to take life so seriously. Ronna and I also had a very special visit to Stonehenge on that trip. We had wanted to go to Avebury but were not able to fit that into our schedule.

After the summer was over, I came back to San Francisco and got a job working as a recruiter for a local staffing agency. I tried to follow my heart and live my life knowing that approval is not essential. The next several years were fertile ground for learning to love myself and to trust my heart and intuition. I made several errors in judgment, especially when it came to matters of the heart. Throughout my twenties I had a pattern of choosing men who were not available. These choices caused unnecessary drama and pain as well as loss of friendship in my life. It was a messy, stressful and drama filled time in my life. I learned from my mistakes and continued to be challenged by my conscious and unconscious desire for approval and acceptance. Reflecting back on that time now, I have much compassion in my heart for my younger self who was doing her best to find her way in the world.

I have spent the last 20 years working with that part of me that wants to be validated by others. I can't say the approval seeking part of me is completely gone, but rather, I am a work in progress. For me, the more I can practice self-love and acceptance, the less I feel the need for approval from others. It has become part of my spiritual practice will probably remain on my radar for the rest of my life.

Any time friends were travelling to the UK, I encouraged them to go to Glastonbury and sit by the Chalice Well and open their heart into the wisdom that is there for them. My niece Lindsay went to Glastonbury in 2000. I sent her to Pandora's Box. It was still there, but had recently changed owners. I wish I had stayed in touch with Jim and his wife Sue, so I could tell them how much they impacted me on that first trip.

It took me twenty years to return to Glastonbury. I was scheduled to be in London for another training and I wanted to spend some time with my friend Jan, who was one of my practice partners in a coaching class. Jan has lived in England for most of her life and had never been to Glastonbury, It was a special treat to be able to share this amazing place with her. We had a wonderful road trip adventure the weekend before my training started. At Avebury we walked amongst the huge stone circle and shared our experiences of the stones. It was good to finally visit Avebury as I had wished on many occasions that I had been able to go years before.

I felt Glastonbury calling to me as we finished up at Avebury. My heart started beating faster as we approached. I felt my heart open as soon as I saw The Tor from the distance. The energy was as magical to me as it was the first time I visited years ago.

We arrived at dusk, had dinner and went to sleep early. The next morning I got to visit the Chalice Well Garden. It felt like coming home. I have heard that if Glastonbury is the heart chakra of the planet, then the Chalice Well Garden is the heart of Glastonbury. As I sat in the garden I realized that I had come full circle. I had just finished my energy coaching training program where I learned to master many of those tools that I learned from Ronna twenty years earlier. I learned how to read energy and turn up the volume on my inner light and essence. The training helped me to understand on a deeper level that the only approval that is essential for me is my own.

My third trip to Glastonbury lasted only 15 hours, but it impacted me on a soul level and brought another spiral of healing to my heart. As I sat in the Chalice Well Garden, I realized that once we fully love ourselves, we have so much more to offer the world. The approval of others becomes so much less important than being aligned and congruent with my essence, or my true self. These realizations shifted me into a deeper alignment with my purpose. Even with this alignment, I know there may still be times ahead of me where I will need to be reminded of the wisdom that Jim shared with me many years ago.

There is something that draws me to Glastonbury. If you have the chance to visit this magical and sacred planetary heart chakra, I highly recommend it. Go there with the intention of travelling along the magical currents. And remember the sage advice from Jim to follow your heart and don't worry about the approval of others.

Kathleen Nelson Troyer *is a heart-based career and life coach. She is the CEO of Jigsaw Staffing Solutions, Inc; where she leads the Career Coaching Division and works on select executive level searches. Gently Moving Forward is the home for Kathleen's private work with clients where she offers individual coaching, facilitates family and systemic constellations and leads transformative adventures and spiritual pilgrimages to sacred spots on our planet. She is a Co-Founder of Essence Coaches, a community dedicated to empowering people to change their lives. She also serves on the board of Heal My Voice.*

Kathleen lives in a seaside cottage with a magical garden about 25 miles south of San Francisco near Half Moon Bay, California with her fabulous husband John and their three cats. She loves to travel, cook, and hike. She is passionate about living a peaceful, joyful and meaningful life.

To contact Kathleen via email: KatTroyer@Gmail.com

www.jigsawstafffing.com www.gentlymovingforward.net

www.essencecoaches.com

www.facebook.com/gentlymovingforward

Story Twelve

The Dance

Holly Eburne

The *Dance* is a beautiful song written by Garth Brooks. The first time I read some of the lyrics was in an obituary in 1988. My son was in kindergarten and a young classmate of his was in a tragic horse accident. She was an only child and her Dad wrote, *"How could I have known you'd ever say goodbye. And now I'm glad I didn't know the way it all would end, the way it all would go. Our lives are better left to chance. I could have missed the pain but I'd had to miss the dance holding you"*.

Every time I experience pain or loss in my life I remember this song. And despite how deep a pain penetrates I wouldn't have missed the dance.

This past week there was a sad situation involving a wounded deer. She was a young doe and was eating from our bird feeders. I shooed her away because there was plenty of natural food in the fields. But she was slow to move. It wasn't long before I saw that her lower jaw was dislocated and hanging loose. When she turned around to look at me, there was a gaping wound on her left forequarter and she was limping. I started crying—in fact it was an ugly cry—because I was helpless to save her. To make the situation worse, there was a coyote circling around. I couldn't watch any longer. This scene, along with red-tail hawks snatching white-crowned sparrows out of sagebrushes, or pygmy owls knocking hairy woodpeckers to the ground, are painful for me. I know predators have to eat but I wish I wasn't around when they did. But...*am I willing to give up the peacefulness and calm that goes along with our country living—just to ease my pain?"* Not a chance.

The dance of owning pets is another one that I wouldn't miss. When I was young, my parents gave away many of our beloved pets--dogs, kittens, rabbits and even a budgie named 'Pretty Pete.' As a child I didn't understand why. The only thing I knew for sure was the deep pain every time it happened. The worst day was when my parents told us that our beautiful standard poodle, Mitzi, was going to another family.

For seven years Mitzi was my soul mate. She was the only one who knew my secret—a secret that I buried for the next 45 years. My Dad was an alcoholic. I hated every day that he came home from his martini lunches because the yelling and screaming would start. There was so much inner turmoil because I was Daddy's girl. He was the one who took care of me when I woke up at night; he was the only one who would comfort me when I was crying in church; and he was the one who took me sailing and to the amusement parks. I felt betrayed and ashamed of our family. I'm not sure how I would have gotten through those painful times if I didn't have Mitzi hiding with me under the bed covers. Or having her curly fur to soak up my tears. On the day Mitzi left our family, I promised myself that when I grew up I would never own a pet. I would never voluntarily put myself through the pain of losing them.

But that promise didn't last long. One day my husband, Dave and our two young children came home with the cutest golden-haired retriever pup named Jake. Dave received him as payment for one of his duck carvings. As soon as they got out of the car and Dave handed me this wiggling little fluffball, I was hooked. He said if I didn't want to keep him, then he would take him back. *Who was he kidding?* Since that day we have never lived without a dog—in fact we have two dogs, two cats, 40 goldfish in our pond, and over 200 wild birds at our feeders. They help me to stay grounded and sane.

And the dance continues...

This morning I was hiking with our spaniels thinking about my life with my husband, Dave. Five years ago he was diagnosed with a rare form of dementia: Frontotemporal Dementia. He was only 57. I wondered if I would have said 'I do' in 1978 if I had known *"the way it all would end, the way it all would go"*. Would I have married Dave if I knew I would become more of a parent, than a partner?

Who knows what my decision in 1978 would have been, but in 2012 I am certain that I wouldn't trade my life for anyone else's. Despite the challenges and pain of slowly losing my husband to an incurable, shameful disease, I wouldn't miss the dance.

For decades, I have studied personal growth but nothing compares to what I'm learning from my greatest teacher—Dave. Twenty-four hours a day he shows me what it means to live in the 'present' moment. He doesn't spend his precious energy worrying about how his disease will progress--the time when he will lose the ability to speak, or get out of a chair; or when he will be incontinent; nor his shortened life expectancy. He is too busy enjoying simple pleasures such as 'finding one more piece' for his jigsaw puzzle, or riding his bike to the bus stop for an adventure into town. And when he walks around town, he isn't embarrassed when former colleagues say hi and he doesn't recognize them. He says, *"I'm sorry I don't remember you. I have Alzheimer's."* (He doesn't remember Frontotemporal Dementia). If Dave has a seizure in a fancy restaurant, or if his clothes look like he slept in them last night, he doesn't worry about what people might think or say. *That's my issue, not his.*

About three weeks after the specialist gave us news about my husband's diagnosis, Dave said to me, *" I may not be able to do anything about my brain dying but I'm going to do everything I can to keep my body healthy"*. I've asked him many times if he is angry that he has dementia and his answer is always the same, *"No. Would that make it any easier?"* Surrendering and accepting 'what is' has been a slow lesson for me.

Watching Dave gives me perspective as he spends hours putting in window screens backwards, or slowly buttoning his coat with fingers that are losing fine motor control. I love how Dave lives without impatience, or drama. So what if we have a power outage and he can't have his morning coffee? Or that he misses a bus and has to wait 45 minutes for the next one? Raising two children taught me a lot about patience but I guess the universe wanted me to learn more from Dave and the challenges of dementia. That is…if I want to do more than just *survive* this journey.

Four years ago I was at the lowest point in my life. Our retirement savings went down in a scam and it slammed me against the wall. *How can I afford help for Dave as his condition worsens? How do I start over in my 50s?* For the first time I couldn't pretend that I was okay. The volume of shame and fear was too much to hide. I could feel my outer shell cracking, and my secrets were seeping through…my life isn't perfect, and neither am I. Finally I admitted that I'm angry over the cards I've been dealt; resentful because this load is heavy, and exhausted from doing it alone; and yes, much sadness over losing my dreams, and my beautiful partner.

But out of the depth of this well comes more peace and love for me—all of me. I am discovering that accepting and loving my darker emotions, not just the happier, lighter ones, means I'm human. Just like you. I am learning to be less critical of myself—therefore of others. I have less shame— therefore more joy. And, I am learning to slow down and live in the present moment with a richer appreciation for the gifts from my sweetest teacher on this planet—Dave.

Just like the song says, "Yes my life is better left to chance. I could have missed the pain but I'd had to miss the dance."

Holly Eburne is a Life & Business Strategist, Physical Therapist, Speaker, & Author. Holly is in the business of helping successful entrepreneurs break through to the next income level by releasing their financial past. Holly uses both a systematic and intuitive approach to coach her clients to a new state of financial abundance. Contact Holly at holly@hollyeburne.com

Part 3

I AM Alive

The whole point of being alive is to evolve into the complete person you were intended to be.

~**Oprah Winfrey**

Story Thirteen

Just Write

Adrienne Yeardye

I am a writer, watching the rise and fall of punctuation, noting the distance between language and its meaning. My message is truth. And in becoming awakened, I have carved out the fear from my own truth, trimmed the fat off my own meaning, and I mean business, marked by words that come through me. What does it mean to be happy?

Near death is relative, as it lies both next door and inside me. Every cell makes its choice in the moment, to multiply or to fold itself seamlessly and silently into the bloodstream, only to be processed indiscriminately by the liver without prejudice. What is and what isn't good for the soul inside a body.

"Every bi-product looks the same to me," says the liver, as it methodically squeezes the good from the bad.

"But what if there is no Joy?" says the Heart, beating between palpitations.

"Then it doesn't matter what you feed me," says the Mind.

And the most interesting part of all this to me, is that I haven't a clue what this means. These are words that came through me, and that I read from my own inner "crystal ball." I have worked so hard to be happy, and it feels so good, so satisfying, so solid. But when I sit on the porch in the sun to have a beer, hands clasped behind my head and leaning back into relaxation, this is the thought that creeps out of my armpit like sweat after a good run. It kind of stinks, but it smells like me. Steeped.

Deciding what to do next in my life is always an issue for me. I know how it ends, and the pieces do fall together naturally, but there is a certain restlessness that continues to exist, as each moment is busily forming the next. To force it to move faster, to deductively create the next moment – a moment is both a single event and a period of time in life, a section, a phase of development – is a fine balance between following an intuitive drawl, and challenging myself to move past the fear and restrictions of my life history. I am out beyond my own streetlights, with no navigational tools to guide me – or limit me. My Intuition is my compass.

When I started this journey ten years ago, I was in search of "controlling" the energy that came into my space. What this initially brought me was Reiki. I answered an ad from a woman who was teaching first level Reiki. I sat in her dark little kitchen, and filled my lungs with her No. 7 cigarettes, one after another, which was something I hadn't done since university. In hindsight, it was a bizarre experience, but at the time, it was strangely enlivening. I let her assure me I was already attuned, and I met with her to exchange treatments for as many times as it took for my own energy to throw her off of me. I remember that moment exactly, a sharpening of the blue haze in the room created a smooth faceless figure on either side of me, and the force of their collective knocked her backwards. The event for me was so impressive; I ignored the black figure that sloped into my room every night, just as I was falling asleep, and stood slumped in the corner. Nightmare after nightmare couldn't scare it away.

The following year I went back to school to become a Homeopath. I drank in the knowledge, and dined hungrily on the words. The homeopathic repertory serves diction as a main course, and for the first time since high school, my abandoned love for words received and gained my attention. This set me apart from others in my field, and I excelled. Nourished, thriving, I took client after client, started a practice and felt my vocabulary return. Obsessive compulsive became fastidious. The way I twirl my hair when I'm anxious became moderate carphologia. And a few clients were lascivious verging on lewd, but strangely that felt like only half of the reason I was there.

And then suddenly there it was. Standing behind his son in my office, was the ghost of a father. Leaning into my ear by satellite, he whispered: "He never did anything fast enough." And by the time I closed my eyes briefly to blink, the homeopathic remedy I needed to prescribe him was written on the inside of my eyelids, in bold.

The feeling that spread over me as this happened was both horror and prowess. It's a captivating feeling, that whispers from the ages of Healer Lore. The first feeling is power and surety, strength. Dare I say truth? I didn't need to look up another word, or ask for another symptom. I knew exactly what the remedy would be, and in the instant that followed, I knew what the treatment would look like also. Cure.

And yet the second feeling was fraud. Who am I to connect a patient to their cure via the back of my eyelids? In homeopathy we have lots of explanations for what is happening in the body, but the Cliff notes state that the remedy connects the Soul to its Maker, and only by that connection healing is created by the physical body, in order to continue the deliverance of Divinity. '

I spent another hour confirming the information. I backed it up, and I hid even from myself that I already knew there was no scientific or credible explanation for how I had received the information, except via Divine intervention, or maybe along the bead of mental illness that may or may not slide itself intermittently, and unreliably, along the river of brain chemicals between nerve endings and receptors.

Schizophrenia is just as much a set of symptoms as arthritis. It starts with quiet and gentle interactions with your own clandestine reality, and it looks a whole lot like Intuition. Perhaps they are varying degrees of the same. In the homeopathic repertory it is classified as "clairvoyance" and considered mental illness.

All dramatic convolutions aside, my stomach churned a red sea of frustration, and if I became still for one moment, I could hear only the scream trapped inside. It pressed my eardrum taught. I wondered sometimes if when my patients walked past me on their way out if they could hear it too. Seashells. I wondered if they felt the perverse boredom of a well-fed cat playing with a mouse. Homeopathy wasn't enough; it became sport. I wondered if my friends felt this too. It became so quick and direct, their cure, that I blurted it out between beers. And as everything in life is always boiled down to its ironic sinew, I lost patients and I lost friends. My practice bankrupted me, and if I had let my own Healer finish her thought, I would have heard my own death approaching at the end of her sentence.

Then, as always, as an answer to my desperate question, "what's next?", my Intuition spoke. I enrolled in an Energy Coaching course, and I loved it. My inner crystal ball was instantly recognized and accepted by my brain. My practice began to build again as I discovered the language that was missing in Homeopathy to connect my patients to the power of their own healing. Energy. Finally, I had a way to explain to them – and to myself – how their physical symptoms were a positive expression, and a map to their energetic imbalances, when re-framed. Suddenly their knee pain blossomed into the key that turned their relationships to themselves around. I could read the energy of the pain, and help them have a conversation with it that resulted in its release. I could prescribe them a remedy to resolve the physical pain. They loved it too, and they began to do better and better. I felt wholly useful. Initially I thought Energy Coaching would enhance their Homeopathy experience, but I quickly saw in my patients that it is the reverse. The energy work they do, holds their remedy longer.

But somehow, somewhere in me, that still wasn't satisfying; I started to get sick again. I felt great, but I knew the symptoms I was beginning to show again were serious. Fortunately, I also knew they were merely energetic at the time, that physical symptoms show up as "feelings" before they become anything irreversible. I closed my Homeopathy practice. It certainly didn't make sense. Financially it was foolish, and I knew it potentially meant career suicide. But I did it anyway; I chose to follow my intuition. I dropped everything and began to focus almost solely on the Energy Coaching program. I participated fully; I did the homework. It tore me to the ground. I received sessions, and gave session after session to classmates and all of my existing clients.

For me, the program did nothing less than resolve my anger with world, starting with animal and mineral, and ending with the blame I had towards my parents about my childhood, my adolescence, and my current adulthood-unfolding. My body ached from the pain I was releasing, but there was no attachment to it. I cried the tears of several life times. I unhooked the cords to my first Love, and I began to feel trust. Most important, I learned to tell the difference between my energy and the rest of the world. It uncovered the truth about me. I was only living half of what I am here to do, but still, I ignored it.

As I started doing more and more coaching, and the hole in my career started to fill up, my finances finally started to improve. It felt amazing. I was living what I had come to believe what was my purpose. My Intuition said: rest. Again, no sense in this, because I was happy. There was nothing to rest about, but I could feel I could only see half of the meaning of this insistent impulse. In hindsight, I would have changed the word to: stay. I definitely felt like a dog, waiting, and I started to get that angry and restless feeling again. I'd had my bone, but only briefly, and I still exhibited the same physical symptoms. No matter what my conscious mind told me, and everyone else, somewhere deep inside of me was not at all happy. I got quiet, and I started to do what I do for my clients. I started to read my own physical symptoms, and let them speak to me in the same way.

What came through me to me both surprised me, and terrified me. I was starving and I wasn't listening. Since I saw so clearly when reading my clients' energies, I had to accept this as both the truth, and as my Divine self-speaking to me, or else. It wasn't a ghost. It wasn't Reiki. And it wasn't a homeopathic remedy printed in bold on the back of my eyelids that would feed me. It was writing - specifically the kind of writing that comes through me from Source. When I see my clients in this way, it's so obvious how impossible it is for them to accept their own answers, and how they create fantastic and fragrant schemes to prevent them with their Mind's reasons for being. I also knew from reading my client's energy that eventually their purpose speaks directly to express the "listen to me or bust" ultimatum. I have relayed this information plenty of times to my clients, and I have physical symptoms to support it, but it was the first time I chose to accept it. To hear the truth meant: if I don't start to live my purpose, my Divine self was going to start looking for another Body with a Mind that was willing to take the more than the proverbial back seat. Is that how I choose it to be? Absolutely not. My Life is a Miracle.

So here I am, half-baked, with all the miscellaneous parts and pieces falling out of my head, and down into my belly to feed me. I don't have a clue where I am going next, but I have made a contract with my Divine self, in reverence to my body, not my details, to write it all down. The truth and nothing but the truth, as it speaks through me, whatever the hell that means.

Adrienne Yeardye is a Classical Homeopath, Energy Coach, and Writer. She specializes in Anxiety and Adrenal Exhaustion, working mostly with women who want to create a satisfying balance between their home and work worlds. An Entrepreneur herself, she understands the joys and the stresses of being the centre of this fulfilling lifestyle. She guides her clients toward creating new and generative connections to their bodies, families, relationships, and businesses. In her own life, Energy Coaching has connected Adrienne to her newest creation – Jupiter's Hive: Stories for Magic People.
www.alternativeoneness.com
www.jupitershive.com

Story Fourteen

Discovering Power in Vulnerability:

Healing the Feminine

Dawn Angeloe

As a child, my favorite moments were being outside in the woods or in a field exploring. I hated wearing dresses and having my hair done into some pretty little girl style. I was fighting being seen as weak. I didn't want to be a girl. I didn't want to be a boy either. I was a tomboy. The power that I felt being myself as a child would not comfortably fit into my family's ideas of what it meant to be a girl. I loved feeling powerful, feeling strong. In all of my immediate and extended family, the idea that women and girls were weak was perpetuated. As a teenager, I was deeply offended when men would suggest to me that I was "pretty enough to be a model." I felt unseen. I wanted to be known for the power of my incredible intellect. I thought that by being seen for having a keen mind would satisfy me.

As a young woman and undergraduate student pursuing a degree in science, I began to experience a gnawing, perpetual feeling of something being absent, an unknown something whose absence was constantly with me. I began to understand I could not continue pursuing a degree in sciences. I felt in the dark about the direction my studies and career were going. I was looking for any ray of light to help guide me. I stumbled upon Women's Studies, which began to change the course of my life. Women's Studies demonstrated to me that undervaluing women and their contribution was systemic in our society, not just in my family. For the first time in my life, I began to see and value myself as a woman. I began to more highly value the women around me and their femininity, and the gnawing of the unknown absence ceased. I began to explore what was pleasurable, what sensuality I enjoyed. But the hard driving masculine had become part of my identity; and even as I explored the value in just being in appreciation, I still became a militant feminist and a militant bisexual.

I finished two degrees and began to pursue a second graduate degree. I had pursued higher education for more than 12 years in multiple graduate programs. And yet, the more highly trained my intellect became, the more dissatisfied with my life I became. It was as if training my mind was causing me to separate myself from who I truly was. That's not to say that the education wasn't important, it was. But it taught nothing about how to really and truly be myself. Endless years of working full time and going to school full time taught me how to ignore what my body needed. I learned how to override the need for sleep, for food, for social connection. I chose to learn to override those needs because I had lost my ability to validate myself. I was driving myself so hard to do, to achieve, and to accomplish so that I could be recognized and validated by others.

From the outside, things looked pretty good. I started a career in clinical psychology. I got married, and adopted a child. But on the inside, I was dying. Despite the progress I had made in my education, in my career, and with building a family, I felt further and further disconnected from myself. The moments of pure joyfulness were few and far in between, and I couldn't figure out why, or what it was that my deep longing was for. I couldn't quite grasp where I had gone wrong, or what I needed to do to help myself.

My training and intellect told me I was clinically depressed. I felt my life was taking me further and further away from who I truly was. I couldn't access the real me. Ironically, I had fulfilled my childhood desire of being recognized for my powerful intellect, a powerful masculine energy, but had lost the connection with my source of inspiration and joy. I had built a life on seeking approval from the outside. Without someone reflecting back to me the progress that I was making or the progress that I was assisting others to make, I felt empty.

One of my closest friends and colleagues recognized my symptoms, despite my half-hearted attempts to conceal them. She called daily to check on me and encourage me. "You need to get on an antidepressant," she would tell me. I would have given the same advice to anyone sitting in my office with the symptoms that I had. I have seen depression take the lives of many people through suicide, and knew that if my symptoms continued, I was at risk of losing my life as well. And yet, I knew medicating myself wasn't the answer. It wasn't just that I had the symptoms. I could feel that I was no longer on the path in my life that I needed to be on to feel deeply satisfied with who I was. I was confused, all the years of training to end up on the wrong path? I was good at what I did, and it wasn't fulfilling me. I began to question my ability to adequately parent. I couldn't connect deeply, meaningfully with the man who I was married to. It felt like everything was unraveling, and I couldn't find the end of the string to weave it back together.

I wanted to fight for my life, but fight who or fight what? I was giving up, surrendering. In desperation, I reached out for an old lover. Feeling the surge of passion through my body, my mind, my being, reignited within me the desire for MY life. The return to my married life was shocking; my marriage no longer fit me either. And yet we had adopted this child together; leaving was not an option. The passion that I had experienced gave me hope that I would again find my way, despite remaining confused about where my path was. Then I began to learn how to see energy, to lift the veil of the obvious and see the wizards behind the curtains. I was immersed in a program that allowed the essence of who I am to be seen by others in the program. I could no longer hide behind any façade, because just as I was learning to read energy, others in the program were learning to read my energy. Through being fully seen by other energy coaches in the program, I began to experience the brilliance of who I truly am. I began a journey back to self-acceptance through being seen and seeing myself more clearly than ever.

I began to understand that the way in which I had lived my life to this point would no longer work for me. By necessity I had lived my life from my masculine side, pushing myself through exhaustion year after year to be able to work full time and go to school full time. I had married a man who was most comfortable being in his feminine energy. He preferred being soft, gentle, and being led in his interactions with others, which resulted in him being too passive in our relationship. And my child had responded better to me when I was in my masculine energy. Through a variety of experiences, I began to reunite with the deliciousness of being completely and entirely in MY feminine energy: being appreciated simply for being me. There was no agenda to fulfill, nothing that I needed to accomplish, I could just be. It was a way of being that I had not experienced until then. My journey back to myself became living more and more from my feminine energy. Much to my surprise, I felt MORE powerful than I had ever felt. I began allowing myself to be enough, without having to accomplish something; and to be in appreciation for myself, my loved ones, and others around me. I felt seen, really and truly seen by others for the first time in my life, while being completely vulnerable. I could feel myself becoming whole. I could feel myself healing.

The world around me began to shift. I was offered a job working in one of the most beautiful places in the country, making more money than I had previously made, doing work that was second nature to me. We moved the family. As I continued to shift into living from the feminine, I became stronger. My child began to respond better to me when I was in my feminine energy. I became gentler, kinder, more accepting, and ever more stronger. My powerful intellect was matched with the powerful nurturing, kind, and gentle energy of my feminine side. I began to experience life as being in flow. There were no more goals to pursue, because just being in the moment was sufficient. Whatever was needed, whatever I needed to do would be brought to my awareness, to my consciousness, in the right moment. I began to trust, really trust in the wellbeing of myself, in the wellbeing of others, and in the wellbeing of the world around me for the first time ever. I began to live my life in collaboration with all of creation. I no longer had to strive, just to be, just surrender, just invite an experience and allow it to be brought to me.

The man who I had married was unable to shift simultaneously into the strength of his masculine energy. The child we adopted began to experience the man who I was married to as weak, then he began to experience himself as weak. He reached out for a lover, and then reached for a life without me, or the child we had adopted, in it. Again, I felt lost. How could this happen? With my skills, my training, my newly acquired ability to see and heal energy, how could I have not prevented this? I watched my child watching me grieve the loss of my marriage, and after more than a week of being despondent, I realized I had to find a way through, so that my child could find a way through as well. If I could find a way to be okay, my child would be okay also.

As I began to feel into the place of surrender, the sweetness began to emerge. The more I surrendered into my life, surrendered into what wanted to emerge for me, and for my child, the sweeter my life became. Yes, there was still bitterness, the bitterness of losing my parenting partner; but the sweetness emerged more and more. And surprisingly, on the other side of surrender was great relief, relief that the last bit of my life that was built on me being primarily in masculine energy had collapsed and crumbled into nothingness. I was free to be me. I no longer had to carry or lead the man who I had married. I no longer had to be militant about anything: not about feminism, not about my sexuality, not about social justice. I had surpassed being militant, and had learned surrender. I had learned how to surrender into me, into life, into the flow. I was free to be me.

The new me is a daily adventure into uncovering who I really am, accepting my true place in the world, and in friendship with myself. The most profound shift for me is that I am boundlessly powerful being firmly rooted in my feminine energy. As I become more fully who I am and more in the moment with myself, the more powerful I become. My world around me continues to shift. Where others find disagreement and feel threatened, I find harmony and endless support. Relationships that had been strained under the fear of being misunderstood and/or abandoned are now blossoming into everlasting friendships.

I am finding within myself the courage to ask for what my heart has been longing for, for nearly a decade. The longing of my heart had been deeply buried due to the belief that I didn't deserve it; I couldn't earn it; and needed to protect myself from the disappointment of wanting something I believed I couldn't have. The courage to ask for the desire of my heart springs from a decided knowingness that I deserve, yes I deserve, and can create what I want in my life; not based on my hard work and endless effort, but just because I choose to be, moment by moment.

Creating what I want in my life does not emerge from the determination of the straightest path from A to B, but from delighting in the pleasure of the moment, that leads to another, and another, and leads me back to me.

Dawn Angeloe *is a psychotherapist and intuitive working with adults and children who are having psychic experiences that they don't understand and may be frightened by, and that may be causing them to secretly wonder if they are going crazy. I help them make sense of their experiences, and teach them skills to be able to manage their gifts. This allows them to have the confidence that they can manage their abilities and make sense of their experiences, so that they able to sleep at night, to no longer feel all alone in their experiences, and to live happier and successful lives knowing they can use their gifts to contribute to the lives of others if they so desire. I can be reached at* ***dangeloe@msn.com*** *or on facebook at* ***www.facebook.com/PsychicShrink****.*

Story Fifteen

The Physical Side to my Love Affair

Meenal Kelkar

I can pinpoint the moment when my love affair began. It snuck up on me … pulled the rug out from under what appeared to be my well-organized life … cleared away the fog. I awakened to long-lost sensation and emotions. For years, the relationship had been based on frustration, annoyance, shame and betrayal. So no one was more surprised than I when out of the blue, a love affair emerged.

Bear with me while I rewind twenty years ago to the beginning of the relationship. I had left my extended family in India and was returning to my husband, dog and home in San

Diego. I boarded the Cathay Pacific plane, exhausted both mentally and physically, as flights traveling abroad leave India at 4am in the morning. As soon as I settled in, I promptly fell asleep against the window, the seats next to me empty. Hours later, I woke up to find a large stranger, sitting in the middle seat, his hand stroking my thigh. As I desperately tried to figure out the best way to take care of myself, I remember thinking, "Keep quiet … No one will believe you … It is your word against his. … All that will happen is he will become angry and it will be worse." So I squeezed myself into the corner of that economy-class seat, trapped, unable to escape, and never said a word. In that moment, I left my Body and began to live my life in my Head.

What I did not comprehend was the collateral damage. You see, in that moment, my libido shut down as well. For these past twenty years, whenever I would begin to feel the inklings of sensual energy within my Body, it would shut down for absolutely no reason. My ability to feel sensation disappeared behind a thick fog of, "Nothing hurts, so everything must be okay." I did not realize that my ability to experience my husband's touch had taken on a superficial quality to it, as if my Body were wrapped tightly in a clear coating that would repel everything and let nothing in. My emotions were dialed way down, as my standard answer to "How are you feeling?" became a habitual, sterile, automated "Good." What I did not know is that my memories of joy and pleasure had taken on the quality of watching a movie, where I could recall the memory, but the associated felt sensation had disappeared. From the inside out, I didn't know that there had been a change, other than the one crucial physical element missing from an otherwise deeply loving relationship with my husband. From the outside looking in, my calm, confident demeanor masked the truth from the experts. If not for my deep knowing that, "This is not how I am meant to live life," I would have been yet another silent victim to my absent libido years ago.

For the next five years, the extent of the damage was hidden by my lifestyle … climbing the corporate ladder, grueling work hours, reaching for that next promotion, striving to make our first house into a home. Doctors would tell me: "Have a glass of wine. All you need to do is relax." At age 30 when we began the talk about having kids, it was obvious <u>that</u> was placing the cart before the horse. Fast forward through 15 years of hormone treatments, psychotherapy, a 10-day intensive for couples at Masters & Johnson, extensive yoga therapy training, acupuncture, an official assessment at UCLA by world-class doctors featured on an Oprah show dedicated to this topic, and I found myself at the edge of 45, no closer to experiencing a break-through in my libido. If you were to ask me how I described my relationship with my Body, "Annoyed, frustrated and helpless" topped the list. "Betrayed" was on the list as well – how could I not be after all of the money I had spent, experts I had seen, techniques I had tried? After all that, what would it take to fix this?! "Ashamed" was the one emotion I refused to admit to, though it has been there all along, lurking behind the scenes. All of this from me! Someone who teaches about the connection between Mind, Body and Spirit!

And then a year ago, I shifted my perspective. I can pinpoint the moment when I was lying on the massage table, listening to my new physical therapist casually mention the phrase "frozen and collapsed", a state in which trauma survivors' nervous systems are often trapped. The more she shared, I realized "She could be describing me!" I can pinpoint the moment because it was as if I had clicked a new lens into place … one where I could see these past two decades of mysterious and commonplace symptoms through the lens of my biology, rather than my biography. I can pinpoint the moment because I shifted from being a victim of my Body to being in partnership with my Body. That's the moment when my love affair began.

Allow me to rewind, and retell my story through this new lens. Unknowingly, I had been living life trapped inside a deep layer of numbness, a word that literally means "deprived of the power to feel or move". The challenge with numbness is that "absence" is the prevalent quality … absence of feeling, absence of sensation, absence of emotion. Numbness looks so much like calm that it can be virtually impossible to recognize. The previous year, I had begun to develop an increasing awareness of a feeling of being tightly wrapped in a clear, impenetrable coating, at times feeling like I was trapped behind a thick invisible wall, unable to experience connection with others. I had learned that deep pain can be hidden behind unconsciousness and numbness, unseen and unfelt. I had already begun to wonder whether there was still another layer to the trauma that I needed to heal. So, in that moment on the massage table, I made the connection, "Frozen. Numb. She could be describing me!"

Yeah, I could be upset that none of those well-paid experts ever guessed the truth of what was going on with me. But I can see so clearly that would have been wasted energy, when my energy was best spent on a quest to learn more about "frozen and collapsed." What I've discovered is that my energy is a precious resource, literally trapped deep within me. Through this new lens of understanding, this is what I now know to be true. In that Cathy Pacific economy-class seat, my nervous system had revved up to 60 miles per hour, my heart began to race, my breathing became shallow and my muscles contracted as I sought to escape the stranger's hand that was pursuing me. Fleeing was quickly eliminated as that meant climbing over my attacker, down a known dead-end into that overcrowded plane. I remember thinking "Keep quiet … No one will believe you … It is your word against his. … All that will happen is he will become angry and it will be worse," a refrain that had unknowingly been locked deep within my subconscious ten years earlier when I was first assaulted at the tender age of 14. So I squeezed myself into the corner of that economy-class seat, trapped like a helpless animal, unable to fight or flee, my voice silenced. I discovered that in that moment, my Body protected me in the only other way possible. Like many trapped animals will do, my Body froze and collapsed, as if dead, in the desperate hope that when I revived, the threat of danger would be gone and I could escape.

Through the gentle, compassionate filter of "frozen and collapsed", my perspective has opened, like a tight bud unfurling into a multi-petaled blossom. I can see now that "sitting there and taking it" wasn't a choice I made, but a biological survival mechanism. I can see now that my 60 miles per hour revved up "fight or flee" energy had a brake slammed onto it, literally trapping all of that energy deep inside of me. I can see now how a seed had been planted within me, so that any time my nervous system entered an aroused state … whether due to stress, anxiety, sensuality, excitement, or fear … my Body would shut down for fear of being overwhelmed. This isn't an excuse for how I've lived my life … this is simply the reason why I've experienced life as I have. There is nothing wrong with me. My Body has been responding in the only way that she has known.

Unwittingly, for all of those years, I had become an accomplice in those long ago violations. In my impatience, running from one expert to the next in order to find the magic button or the magic pill, in commanding my libido to "Jump" and feeling annoyed by the lack of immediate reaction, I had been perpetuating the cycle of violence against my Body by my thoughts and behaviors. In believing my story that "I sat there and let it happen", I was quietly and viciously beating myself up. Slippery, slimy, stinky Shame was trapped deep within the recesses of my Body along with my long-sought libido. It was so much easier to get caught up in the socially acceptable pattern of Overworked Overwhelmed Overachiever than to sit with the dark, silent, numb, unseen corners of my Being. I can see now how that urge to fight or flee had defined my relationship with my Body for twenty years.

And that is the key. As long as I was resisting, pushing, controlling, demanding or fleeing, the "frozen and collapsed" pattern remained locked in place … my energy trapped deep within a thick wall of numbness … so far out of reach that I couldn't even see it, let alone feel it. What I learned on that massage table is that with "frozen and collapsed," anything more energetic than stillness, patience and compassion will cause the nervous system to contract even more tightly. Just like the cornered wounded animal that doesn't know you, slow movements, patience, a soft voice, a gently outstretched hand and tenderness are what work best to invite frozen to thaw and collapsed to expand. In that moment, when my perception shifted, and I understood the biology of my trauma, my love affair with my Body began.

I began by asking myself questions: "How would it be to love and appreciate all that my Body has done for me?" "How would it be to offer that same patient, loving tenderness to my Body as I would to a frightened, wounded animal?" "How would it be to slow down and truly listen to what my Body has been telling me she needs for so long, in the only way that she knows how?" "How would it be to accept and celebrate my Body as a wise partner in doing this thing called Life?" Truly accepting and taking action on my answers scared the breath right out of me because I could see they meant I had to slow down, something I had absolutely no skill in doing after spending decades perfecting Overworked Overwhelmed Overachiever. And yet, I knew that I had to take a step, any step, down this path because I knew deep within that this would lead me to a very different outcome from all of my previous attempts. For a change, I needed to be the driver in my Life ... the expert of my own Experience ... the lover of my Body and my Being.

Thus began my quest to find those parts of myself that I could not see or feel because they had been trapped behind the wall of numbness. You may wonder, "How do you find the presence of absence?" I did it by following a saying from my yoga therapy training, "Yoga is the practice of bringing the light of consciousness to the unconscious." So I sought to discover those areas of my life where I had gone unconscious. And I was astounded by the depth and breadth of my numbness. The depth of my physical numbness was revealed when my massage therapist leaned into a knot of tension in my hip for several long moments and I couldn't feel a thing. I even had to ask, "Is there a knot there?" That is how absent sensation had been for me. Thereafter, I began to speak out loud whenever I noticed sensation of any kind during my massage in order to re-establish the link between my Mind and the truth of what was going on within my Body. Through regular massage, I discovered that my ability to experience my husband's touch had taken on a superficial quality to it, as if my Body were wrapped tightly in a clear coating that would repel everything and let nothing in. That is how flat my experience of Life had been.

Thereafter, I developed a vocabulary to describe the quality of sensation that I was experiencing so that I could discern the difference between "nothing" and the varied richness of "something." Then, I discovered that my memories of joy and pleasure had taken on the quality of watching a movie, where I could recall the memory, but the associated felt sensation had receded into the fog. That is how thick the foggy layer of numbness had been. Thereafter, I chose each week to prioritize seemingly mundane activities that I knew I experienced as either "full-bodied," "awaken my senses," or "filled with joy." For me, these included watching dogs romp in the park, walking on the beach, or visiting a farmer's market to seek out fresh vegetables and fruit. Each choice was a chance for my Body and my Mind to reinforce a fresher, deeper, more vivid neural net of joy and pleasure.

Similar to the "pins and needles" sensation that happens when the part of your Body that has fallen asleep begins to wake up, I began to experience discomfort as well. Through the support of regular bodywork and yoga classes, I began to experience twinges, wobbles and stumbles in yoga poses that had always come easy to me. I felt shocked to discover that my physical strength and sure-footedness was directly tied into the rigid tension interwoven within my shoulders, hips and pelvis. That is how thick the armor had been in my Body.

Thereafter, I chose to approach my yoga practice as if I were a beginner, showing up for the first time in my continuing-to-transform Body. In doing so, I could pay close attention to placement and positioning, thereby strengthening parts of my Body unfelt and unknown for two decades. I smiled and said "thank you" with each wobble and twinge to celebrate with my Body as she released yet another piece of that numb, tightly-laced tension. I began to notice that I would often power through my day or find myself firmly in overwhelm or at the most extreme, thoroughly depleted. I understood that these patterns were a sign that I was kicking up my "fight or flight" response as a source of energy, rather than relying on my emerging life force energy. I felt dismayed to discover how prevalent these patterns were in my life … that the overachiever in me had perfected overworked and overwhelmed! <u>That</u> is how deeply hidden my life force energy had been within my Body. Thereafter, I chose to become an overachiever in noticing whenever I felt activated. In that moment of noticing, choice emerged. "Do I continue down this route that I know so well? Or do I pause, take a breath and ask myself "what can I change here?" I discovered options that had been there all along, but unseen because I had been running through my life at 60 miles per hour. Admittedly, some options, like saying "No", were extremely uncomfortable, but it had become a matter of life and death for me. Say yes to new life enriching patterns or continue in what I now knew had been life depleting ones? While the choice seems obvious, at the time it was a moment-by-moment practice of remembering and choosing aliveness over numbness.

Within this new enlivening chapter of my Life, my Body began to rewire herself and I feel excited to write that my previously deeply trapped life force energy has begun to emerge, along with my libido. It is a year later and I wish I could tell you that everything is perfect. Honestly, I find myself in transition, like a caterpillar transforming with the deep down knowing that the butterfly <u>will</u> emerge. I wish I knew when that will be, but I don't. And yet I can see evidence of tremendous change and inklings of what can emerge from these fresh, fragile Self-Full habits. To stay on track, I must be vigilant in sifting through the elaborate stories that my Mind creates, worthy of any soap opera writer, so that I can distinguish reality from fantasy. For example, three times in three months, I was able to ride the gentle rise and ebb of my libido without shutting down. In the past, my Mind would create this story: "Yeah, but when will I ever reach the Holy Grail and have an orgasm?" In that self-defeating perspective, I'm beating myself up again for not being good enough, fast enough, skilled enough. I know where that path leads and I am done with that! So here is my rewrite, coming from that place of partnership with my Body: "Prior to this love affair, freely riding the wave of my libido had happened <u>only</u> once in 20 years. And now it has happened three times in three months! WOW!"

I never dreamt that I would be challenged to revisit my perception of myself on so many levels… to love my Body so deeply that I can even celebrate wobbly footing as evidence of my transition from "frozen" into "aliveness." Much to my surprise, I find myself enveloped in a deep sense of wonder … wonder at the tenacious strength in which my Body has held on to this trapped energy in an effort to protect me … wonder that my Essence has deemed that <u>now</u> is finally the time for this layer of the trauma to come to the surface and be released … wonder that I've held onto it just so I could learn to be compassionate, loving and self-nurturing with myself. I can pinpoint <u>this</u> moment when my love affair with my Body deepens, as I experience a moment of knowing the fullness of myself with more richness and vibrancy than I ever thought possible.

PS. You can learn more about "frozen and collapsed" through Peter Levine's Somatic Experiencing.

Meenal Kelkar *is a Transformation Coach and certified Yoga Therapist. Her journey has taken her from Fortune 500 companies to growing her own Mind-Body-Spirit business, where she teaches Overworked Overwhelmed Overachievers how to break free of the stress-burnout cycle in order to tap into a more vibrant, sensual experience of life. Meenal's commitment to her newfound life force energy led to an on-line version of her popular Mpowerment Meditations course. She finds herself in transition, having left behind an energy-depleting approach to life, and is now exploring, "What gets my juices flowing?" You can find Meenal at* **www.Integrative-InSight.com** *and* **www.EssenceCoaches.com**

Story Sixteen

Falling Into Place a Midlife Journey

Marilyn O'Malley

We are all influencing each other whether we are aware of it or not. What matters is what you choose to follow, see and allow yourself to experience.

In 2005, an old friend contacted me on the Internet after 25 years of absence. I was curious about why Tom would search me out after all these years. After much consideration, I determined his gift of connection was to remind me of my adventuresome self. Just thinking about living fearlessly, being curious and spontaneous got me excited and day-dreamy.

The next day my daughter called and said she wanted to check out schools in California over spring vacation. Before my reminder from Tom, I would have hemmed and hawed, but instead I stayed with the adventurer feeling and said "YES, but only you and I are going!"

A couple weeks later, Caitlin and I were driving on the coast highway from L.A. to Santa Barbara. As soon as we came into the expansive view of the ocean, sky and mountains I felt myself breathe in more deeply than I had in a long time. I felt free! We stayed with a welcoming college friend and his family. I found myself full of gratitude and warmth in my soul as I walked the beaches barefoot, smelled the ocean air, watched surfers ride the waves and felt the mountain energy sooth my New England winter body. I felt naturally comfortable here, like I'd come home. More than my home in Mystic, CT where I have lived the last 20 years raising a family and building a life. I finally had the feeling of being home.

My daughter commented on how everyone was so friendly and smiles. This reminded me: When I first moved back east, I had new friends tell me I couldn't smile as much, because New Englanders wouldn't trust me. I had to turn down my natural enthusiasm for life or not be trusted in my new home. At the time it felt like a no brainer. Don't smile as much to be accepted. I'm sure from that point forward I tried to match "New England mannerism" to fit in, leaving parts of me feeling abandoned.

Back in Santa Barbara, without the imaginary boundaries of New England and my husband, I felt free to turn my light up. My New England façade was thawing and my free spirit, happy roots were becoming exposed. I experienced how much I had been denying my true self-expression, even as simple as losing my smile.

After Santa Barbara, we went to San Diego to see my mother and friends. While I was there I kept getting comments from friends I visited about an old boyfriend, named Peter. Multiple times there were comments, Peter this and Peter that. I thought what is up? I didn't really think he wanted to see me, as he was married with two children and we hadn't connected with each other in 25 years.

Peter and I grew up together in Coronado, a town in the San Diego area, but we didn't date each other till I was in college. By then we didn't live in the same town. I was in Santa Barbara and he lived in Lake Tahoe. We would get together for weekends when we could.

In 1979, I was moving to San Francisco to attend a new

college to study parapsychology and I felt like I wanted to make a bigger commitment with him. He was moving back to San Diego for work. No cell, the only way to reach him was his family's home phone and he was never there when I called. After many attempts to catch him, one of his brothers definitively tells me, "Peter doesn't want to see you and stop calling!" I assumed Peter was getting my messages and his unreturned calls were proof his brothers comments were the truth.

I was hurt and felt like Peter and I had unfinished business. So for the next 25 years, at least once a year, I'd have a dream about him. I'd arrive at a party and someone would tell me Peter is in the next room and I'd go to find him in the crowd of people only to find out at the other end of the house that he was already gone. I would wake up frustrated.

On the last day of my trip, I was visiting my mother in Coronado and the day events kept oddly changing. A part of the plan had been to say good-bye to mom after our lunch at the Hotel Del Coronado and go back to my friend's home in San Diego for dinner. Instead, Jeanette called me and said she and her son were driving to Coronado, so why didn't we have dinner there. I changed my plans and said, "Okay!"

A few hours later, my mother, Jeanette, her son and I are eating dinner on the patio next to the sidewalk when Peter walks by the restaurant. He doesn't live in Coronado now, so this is a chance encounter. "Oh my God," my heart is pounding. What do I do? If I go out now I may never come back to the table. I remind myself he may not want to see me. What if there is still chemistry? I set a marker, if he is still there after we all finish dinner, then it is meant to be and I will say hi. It took us another 20 minutes to finish and when I walked out, there he stood.

I stepped forward vulnerably and said, "Hi Peter" and he looked at me with his head straining forward trying to make sure what he was seeing was real. It felt like such a long time with no response I thought, "do I need to say my last name?" But, as he slowly moved toward me I could feel a tremendous amount of love pouring out of his eyes and heart. This startled me. It was only seconds but it felt like forever and all the sounds around me were on mute until he spoke and then I noticed my mother, Jeanette and her son staring at us.

After firing questions at me, "How long are you here for? When can I see you? I need to see you!" we scheduled a meeting at a coffee shop the next morning before my flight back home with my daughter.

The next day Peter walked into the coffee shop with a baseball cap on over a baldhead, 50 pounds heavier than the hard body, blond, longhaired surfer I was in love with 25 years ago. And yet, his energy still excited me and I felt like I was eighteen years old again. The first thing he said to me was, "Why did you leave me? You were my soul mate." Totally confused and blown away, we both figured out that Peter's brother never told him I called and he never was one to pursue.

As we talked, my life force energy came back into me like it hadn't been in a long time. I literally felt a click go off in my brain, just like someone turned on a light switch, and I knew I was going home and leaving my husband. I could no longer live my life with my light turned down. I thought I was drying up and aging because of peri-menopause, but at that moment I realized how I had been feeling was a result of what I had been willing to settle for in my life. I realized at that moment with Peter, I was no longer willing to settle for less of anything in life. I felt the juices of my life flood through me. **I am alive! I choose to live my life fully!**

I couldn't live a lie. I couldn't be the wife, the mother, the life coach, the friend I wanted to be and live the lie I was living with my husband. I needed to be able to be vulnerable, authentic and be celebrated. I needed to be able to express myself without feeling wrong for being different than my husband. I didn't love him as a wife anymore. To continue this journey was harmful for not only me, but as a role model for my children. My spirit was dying in this relationship.

When I returned home, I shocked my husband and my friends noticed a change in me immediately. I felt so alive, vital, frisky and with unlimited possibilities. I wanted to hear music all the time and I felt like dancing.

I teetered between an orgasmic life rush and heart gripping fear of the unknown as I transitioned through the struggles of leaving 20 years of my life invested in a community, friendships and a marriage. I had to deal with my husband's anger and humiliation, friends confusion, children's reactions, the uncertainties and fears of others, as well as my own. I had to deal with my guilt of breaking up a home. I knew I was turning our lives upside down and inside out and at the same time I needed to put myself first this time and decide what I had to bring to my game of life.

I wanted my children to see what a healthy, respectful and deeply caring relationship was like. I wanted them to know that they could be in a relationship where they could fully express who they are and be celebrated. I wanted them to know sacrificing yourself is not an option. I wanted them to know you're never stuck. I wanted them to know they are responsible for creating how they feel about their life.

I was leaving my husband. I never thought I would do that. We had been together for 24 years after meeting and both feeling called to each other. I remember the sensation of a hand coming out of my gut and taking hold of a hand out of his gut. At that time, I knew I was marrying him and we would raise a family together. When we married, I made a commitment to him for life. I believed we would grow old together with our family and friends. Over time it became apparent that our definitions of an intimate relationship were different. I kept thinking I was doing something wrong. I kept thinking it was all my fault. If I become a better lover, better communicator, smarter, and etc., we would have the connection I desired. Jerry considered my dissatisfactions of the relationship, my problem. I worked on bettering myself and from my efforts I grew and learned a lot about relationships. I learned I can't change him I can only change me. All I was hoping for was for Jerry to grow with me. Instead what happened was we grew apart.

I want to make it clear: I didn't leave my husband for Peter. I left him for ME. Thankfully the timely email from Tom and the in-person conversation with Peter woke me up and reminded me who I AM.

Exiting my marriage, I set out on a midlife journey leaving my security and comfort behind to face my biggest fears while becoming more of me. Fulfillment, living my big dreams, celebration, happiness, deep connections, successfully serving and expansion of love for others and myself was what I aimed for. I was scared but at least I would live or die moving in that direction. Jerry was right, it wasn't about him, it was about me all along. I still thank him for all the opportunities he provided for me to grow.

Scared to death and yet feeling some confidence, I felt called to move back to Santa Barbara where I knew I was resourceful enough to make the transition. I didn't know how, but I knew where I was headed was healthier and more in alignment with my truth than where I was at the moment. I had to find my faith in myself and in the universe.

When I would wake up at three in the morning with an anxiety attack about money and worrying about how I would support myself, I would say, "STOP! What do you want?" I'd get clear and ask the universe, " if I'm not meant to do this, then make it very clear to me and show me the way with ease and grace. Then I'd go back to sleep. And the next day I would open up to me with ease and grace in between the heart pounding fears. Each day I grew my faith and love for myself. Eventually, I could sleep through the night.

I've learned my life is about who I am, not about my personal "stuff." My faith in the universe and in myself allows me to walk with uncertainty towards my challenges and use my creative expression to develop solutions. I had to discover who I was without all my comforts, learning to be with my pain, so I could find my way to saying **"yes"** to life instead of **"no"** out of fear. This takes time and it has been an amazing journey. I could not have imagined the life I live now had I stayed in CT, with my husband.

Some say it took great courage for me to leave my comfortable position to seek greater happiness. It did and it took me knowing what I really desired from my life. I had to know deep in my soul why I was leaving my husband and moving across the country away from all my friends. My friends weren't leaving their husbands and they had some of the same complaints I had. Friends and family were questioning my sanity. I had to know what the value of leaving was for my future.

This journey required me finding support and learning

the ability to ask for help. I had friends offer money if I needed it, friends who listened, mentors who were teaching me about my power, and friends who celebrated my need to go out into the world and express myself differently. My second day in Santa Barbara, I joined a networking group that felt like a family and supported me every Thursday morning to feel connected to my new life.

I realized I could sink or swim by my choices. I was no longer co-dependent. I had to redefine how I saw myself and be the new me. I had been the wife and mother for 20 years and all that involved. I had to grieve the loss of my relationship to my husband and the family environment I had created for us all. I had been thinking I wasn't enough for my husband and now I knew I could be more than I imagined. I could no longer afford to see myself as not enough.

To manage the fears I created plans with back up strategies in order to feel confident. Even though I moved very quickly I had plans A, B, and C and would remind myself when fear reared its ugly head that there wasn't only one solution. If something went wrong there were many solutions. My trusty intuition guided my decisions leading me to my homes, meeting key people, and a new life partner. I made up what I wanted to believe about my life and all the possibilities. I meditated, exercised, and connected with others. For me to be ME required I show up in alignment with my truth as it was revealed to me.

All the expectations I had for leaving have fallen into place in my life and so much more than I ever imagined! Three years into my transition, I was driving home from a two-week road trip with my life partner, Jeff, and all of a sudden I started crying because it hit me that I had everything that I wanted. I was in a relationship with a man who understood and valued me. We were adventurous and I spent lots of time in nature. I experienced my value as a life coach and I was happy. Jeff and I now shared a home with our cat Prince Philip. We lived across from a park, that sits on top of a cliff, where I can watch dolphins, whales and birds pass by. I have helped create incredibly supportive and dynamic communities in my life, filled with magnificent women, energy readers and healers.

I have only benefited from my choice to leave as I continue to learn to define my life and overcome my obstacles.

In my unraveling, I revealed my personal power and my essence. The process of this journey has bared an intuitive, strong, adventurous, courageous, vulnerable, resourceful, leader and creative woman whose life is falling back in place.

I AM HOME.

Marilyn O'Malley is the founder and co-creator of Essence Coaches, LLC, a co-creative community dedicated to empowering billions of people to change their lives. Marilyn is dedicated to working with entrepreneurs and leaders who are READY to own their power, magnificence and to influence the world without sacrificing themselves.

www.EssenceCoaches.com,
www.MarilynO'Malley.com

Story Seventeen

Going Into the Dark to Find the Light

Charlene Sansone

Most mornings I wake up and wonder how I got here.

When I say here, I mean....
...42
...flat broke
...$25,000 in debt
...no consistent income flow
...no luck finding work
...single
...living with my parents
...and little to no motivation or joy around life.

I never imagined it would be this way and honestly, I

just don't feel like myself.

What happened? Where did I go? How do I get myself back?

The time I remember most fully experiencing what I would consider me was when I was producing commercials for advertising agencies. I loved taking something from pictures and words on a piece of paper to a tangible, visible, real life experience and communication. I loved the creative and collaborative aspects of it. It exercised the best of both my worlds... my intuitive, creative self and my grounded, logical and analytical self. And somehow when those two came together... there were fireworks.

The other part I remember is, as much as I loved it, there were times I hated it. The landscape of the ad world was changing. The standard print, outdoor, broadcast and mail strategies were becoming obsolete. The amount of media outreach channels exploded. With that, ad agencies were no longer the experts and advertisers had to spread the same budget across the many and varied channels that were emerging. For me, as a producer, this netted difficult demanding wishy-washy clients, agencies jumping to meet their changing needs in order to keep their business and I was run ragged to continually execute it all, typically with unrealistic time frames and budget expectations. Needless to say, I worked long and arduous hours and handled a high amount of stress. Somehow I managed it all with a smile on my face.

I will never forget when my first Executive Creative Director called me into her office to appreciate my work and tell me she heard I was unshakeable. I don't know who it was but someone mentioned to her that I handle the worst of situations with a smile on my face and an unbelievable amount of calm. I thanked her for the compliment yet something about what she was saying just didn't compute because that is not what I felt on the inside.

It wasn't until I heard this time, and time again from others that I began to notice it myself. No matter how bad things got, I had a smile on my face. And finally I realized the bigger the problem, the bigger the smile.

Truthfully, smiling comes very naturally and

authentically to me. And also, there are times when it is not; it just looks like it is.

This goes back to something my mom told me when I was a child, which was "put a smile on your face and you will always feel better." So I did, I put a smile on my face in honor of feeling better. But guess what.... It didn't work. As I said before, it just looked like it did. What really happened is, I tried so hard to feel good through my smile but couldn't.... I stopped feeling.

When I first heard the phrase "emotionally repressed," I wondered if that was me. Now looking back, I know that was a little wink from the heavens pointing me to a pertinent clue on my path.

I wasn't a happy child or at least that I can remember. To be honest, my childhood was not good and I do not have very many memories from it. You would think I would remember birthday parties, holidays, vacations, my first day of school... stuff like that. And I don't. It is mostly a blur and has more of a feeling tone... predominantly terrified, sad, anxious and angry.

The earliest memory I do have is me crying in my crib one night until my mom came home from work. She worked at night so she could be home while my dad worked during the day. I could not wait to see her. She came in, calmed me down and rubbed my back until I fell asleep. This became a regular thing. I am not sure the crying was regular but I know I often kept myself awake until she got home. It continued for many years... her working at night and me not sleeping until she came home... because I also remember being in bed wrapping the covers all the way around my head, to leave only my face showing so I could breathe, waiting, watching every shadow reflecting on the door of my room and in the hallway and listening for the front door to open and close so I knew she was home. It was then, that I felt safe enough to go to sleep.

I didn't feel safe at all with my father. He had a horrible, terrifying temper and would pop off in an instant, into a rage, turning beat red in the face, screaming at the top of his lungs, shouting obscenities and it was often directed at my mother, even if it wasn't about her. It was a scary thing to

173

witness and at those times anyone or anything in his vicinity ended up mentally, emotionally, spiritually and energetically crushed by the rage. I hated it when it happened and after a while, I began to hate him.

Can you see why putting a smile on my face to feel better might not exactly work?

The rages started when I was very young. As a matter of fact, I know it started before I was born. My parents tell a story about this huge fight they got into on their honeymoon. They were at a lake resort fishing and the whole place could hear my dad's screaming echo across the lake and through the cottages. That evening the owner's young son showed up with a fresh bowl of popcorn encouraging them to make up... especially as newlyweds.

Also, in my efforts to heal myself over the past few years, I was taken back to being a fetus in my mother's womb and instantly felt an overwhelming amount of sadness and resentment. Very rarely do I cry that hard. As a fetus in the womb, I was sad and resenting the choice I made to be born to these people who were in so much turmoil and unhappiness. And I was also feeling the sadness and resentment of my mother for the situation she was in and the choices she had made. Ironically (or not), I was born three weeks late.

As I began to grow older, become more myself and more aware, the hate started to turn into anger. By eight years old, I was declaring that I had, had enough and would stand up to my father and defend my mother. It didn't work very well. It only made him more defensive and didn't help my mom's situation. But I was angry and didn't really know how else to handle it other than what I was doing.

There is one time I remember being at my grandparent's house. I am not sure if it was for a holiday or the typical Italian "anyone who can make it comes," Sunday night dinner with the family. As usual, to show his power, especially in front of people, my dad degraded me for absolutely no reason at all. I didn't deserve it, so I got angry and answered back. I know I ended up in tears and have a vague memory of my mother pulling me into the laundry room to tell me not to do that. I never forgot how I felt... my heart shattered and I felt absolutely powerless. I got scolded from both sides and began to take in that I was a very bad girl who needed to learn to control herself and her emotions.

The whole entire coping mechanism in my family was about numbing and pretending everything was OK, when it really wasn't. We danced or more like tip toed around my father and his explosive anger and negativity. My mother internalized it all and found that it was easier to depend on and control me, and my brother, better than him and his emotions. So that became the strategy.

So, I did my best. I didn't want to disappoint her or let her down. She had enough problems as it was being married to my father, taking care of the household including all the financial aspects and juggling a million balls to keep it all looking together. I wanted to lighten her load, not increase it. So, I bought in and did my best to stay in. The only way it worked is to stuff my feelings down and turn them off. It didn't happen instantly. It took practice... many years of practice. Sometimes I fell off the wagon and the pain it caused to express how I really felt when my dad was being "my dad" and the crushing, absolutely demeaning, condescending responses I received from him made it easy to get right back on, stuffing it all down and numbing it all out again.

What I have learned over the years of my life journey is that when you numb (or deny) the pain you also numb (or deny) the joy. Before I really understood this I would commend myself for the amazing amount of "neutrality" I had. I was always in the middle, never to one extreme. I was really proud of myself and it worked for me. Until...

Fast forward to a woman in her mid thirties, producing commercials for ad agencies, struggling to grow, getting burnt out, finding herself called to a life of more meaning and a growing desire to live authentically with purpose and passion. That woman was me.

I was no longer inspired by the work of producing commercials like I was when I first started out. And there was no career path in the ad world I wanted to pursue. The summer before I quit, I worked everyday and every weekend to produce a package of spots for 1.3 million dollars that never aired. What I knew is that I wanted, and was being called, to do something else. At the time, my life was so filled with deadlines, tight schedules, large "to do" lists, and making things happen, I could not discern what. So, I quit the ad world in October of 2005 to find out.

At the time I left, I did not know I was so numb and in such deep denial, so how could I realize the struggle, burnout and stagnancy was 100% related to it.

Actually, it wasn't until last year while having dinner with a friend and listening to him tell me his story that I began to see and unravel my own dysfunction. The sentence he said that hit me like a ton of bricks was, "I was walking around like everything was OK and it really wasn't. I was leading a double life." I instantly knew that was me too. I suddenly became aware of how deeply depressed, confused, empty, and broken I felt yet, was still pretending to be completely fine every day. When I talked with my family, friends, old colleagues or anyone, I acted as if I had it all handled because there was a huge wall of numb and denial in-between the truth and myself. I couldn't feel how upside down my life was. Not ever. That is how I survived.

As the wall started coming down and truth started to rear it's ugly head, there were a few days that I had overwhelming feelings of not wanting to be here anymore. Yes, I do mean suicidal. I felt like there was no reason for me to be alive any more. I could not connect to purpose, or meaning and truly believed that no one would be affected if I left this life. I would look out my window at the huge, beautiful tree in my front yard and recognize it as so, yet still lay back in bed and pray to be taken from this earth and my pain.

During one of those times, I finally decided to call a healer friend and ask if she would be willing to offer me a healing because I desperately needed help. Of course, she said yes and did it remotely that evening. We began the session on the phone for a few minutes to connect and during that time, she asked if I was ever sexually abused. I answered "not that I remembered." At that moment, I didn't know how important that question and my answer was going to be in fully breaking through to the other side.

This brings me to the end of 2011. I am giving it all I got and still coming up dry. Yet, feeling some sort of excitement to wipe the slate clean and start over for the New Year. And not only the New Year, but also the infamous year of 2012. It is to be the end, the beginning or both. At this point, any thing other than my current circumstances sounded good to me.

One thing I didn't mention is that I spent all of 2011 learning to be an energy coach. So, to prepare for this auspicious year of 2012 consciously, one of my classmates and I decided to trade sessions with each other on December 31st. I asked about the pattern of job potentials that came into my life and never came to fruition. The result of that was, I was not moving from 100% clarity and truth, which completely made sense to me. I really didn't want the jobs. I was just applying for them because that is what I know how to do and I needed the money. Again, denying my true feelings.

A few days later I was doing another practice session with a classmate and had shared about the previous session. She asked me if I wanted to find out what was keeping me from moving from my clarity and truth. Of course I enthusiastically said yes!!! As she read my energy, she saw a box that was locked and there was something very sacred in it. Energy presents itself symbolically so it was as if something was locked up inside me, interestingly enough, it was located right below my heart. I wanted to know what was inside. So, she coached me into communicating with the box and it wasn't working. She said that it looked like it would take some nurturing and with that comment, I actually got mad. One of the ways to transform energy is to talk to it and in my anger I said, "I am not talking to a box for 21 days to see what is in side. No way!" I then asked her what it would take to open the box immediately. The answer was – implicit TRUST.

Within 24 hours, the box opened itself. I happened to be talking to another friend on the phone about something else and she asked me the question of "were you ever sexually abused?" I had heard this question very recently before, and I wondered why was it coming up again?

In an instant, it all came to me. Was I going to lie again and continue in denial or was I going to tell the truth? The weird thing about it is, on some level, up until that moment, I didn't remember I was lying. I actually made it my reality that I could not remember that I was doped and raped in college. As I said," Yes I have," in one moment the house of cards fell. I not only saw, in a flash, the incident but every other violation of self that occurred in my 42 years of life. There was a rush of emotions.... anger, sadness, blame, shame, denial, utter self-worthlessness and more sadness. You would think I would be upset about the person who violated my body and my space but that is not what I was feeling. It was a deep sadness for the girl who picked herself up off the floor and walked home bare foot, relieved that her roommate wasn't home so she wouldn't have to explain. I was sad for the girl who blamed and shamed herself for letting it happen. I was sad for the girl who didn't feel safe enough to tell a soul and locked it all away, as if it never happened, never to be discussed (until 22 years later). I was sad for the girl who felt that what happened and how she felt didn't matter.

And the biggest rush of sadness came as I realized, this one event represented the entirety of my life up until now. Numbing and denying my feelings, my expression and who I am, in essence, is a deep violation of myself, akin to rape... as if I had raped myself. For a moment I couldn't believe I had actually done that to myself and then the truth set in.... I had, and that is exactly how I got "here."

Yet simultaneously, inside the pain of that awareness came the joy of understanding the way from "here," to the "there" I have been dreaming of, reaching for and feeling so far away from.

Now, I know exactly how to get myself back and am on my way…

Charlene Sansone, *lives in Glen Ellyn Illinois. She is an event and media producer by trade. At heart, she is a visionary seer/planetary midwife, here to birth the next evolution of the planet and humanity. She plays many roles... teacher, healer, guide, communicator, orchestrator, whatever else she is called to do and speaks to her heart. Her hobbies include yoga, reading, hiking, biking, traveling, the ceremony of food and drink, being a perpetual student of life, humanity and the human condition, deep, meaningful, engaging conversation, and spending quality time with family and friends. And, laughter... lots of laughter!! She can be reached at* **charlenesansone@gmail.com***.*

http://walkingintouncertaintywithcertainty.wordpress.com/

Part 4

I AM Beauty

"I don't think of all the misery but of the beauty that still remains."

– Anne Frank

Story Eighteen

My Journey Back to Love

Maryann Hesse

"I don't think we should see each other anymore. I just don't love you anymore." Hearing those words sent shock waves through my body and my stomach began to churn. I felt like I was going to vomit. The words were reeling in my head as he drove me home and walked me to my door.

All of a sudden, the porch light flew on and a girlfriend opened the door to my house from inside. She had stopped by to visit and wanted to welcome my boyfriend back from his trip to Europe that summer.

I was furious! I pushed past her and shut off the light and slammed the door shut. How dare she invade these last precious (in my mind) moments I had with him after his announcement to me!

That was the beginning of a type of hell that I swore, at age 16, I would **never** go through again!

The next few days were a blur. I was like a robot on automatic pilot. I would sit down to dinner with my parents and force myself to eat. I said very little but then in my house no one said much anyway. My parents were emotionally distant from each other and from me, their only child. Mostly, I don't think they had a clue what to do with me. They never had. I didn't fit the "mold' of the obedient farmer's daughter. I had an adventurous spirit and it didn't mesh well with these traditional Iowans who had never lived far from where they grew up.

Back then there were no counselors or therapists like today and my girlfriends were at a loss as to how to help me through this. It wouldn't have mattered. I had withdrawn inside myself. It felt like I was wrapped in a cocoon of pain, my own private hell—a prison cell. It was surreal on some level. I had sentenced myself to a life in my own solitary confinement.

During the next three months my menses ceased completely. My body was in such stress, and distress, that it just stopped functioning correctly. My mother, with whom I was never able to talk much about anything, jumped to the conclusion that I must be pregnant.

At that time I had no idea how that happened between two people but in my twisted thinking it seemed somehow like a possible 'link' to my ex-boyfriend. There in my quiet desperation was perhaps a ray of hope in some sick way that could have him pay a little attention to me again, a way to connect with him somehow.

This made no logical sense but who was logical at this point? Certainly not me. So off I went to a doctor's office to get an examination. Of course, he found nothing. Oddly enough, no one bothered to explain 'the facts of life' to me even after this whole ordeal.

That event permanently colored the way I saw relationships. I went off to college, a rebellious hellion, acting out in outrageous ways, experimenting with drugs trying to understand somehow the world my ex had suddenly disappeared into. (His trip to Europe had been with college kids, even though he had just finished his junior year in high school. They had exposed him to a whole new world—one of sex, drugs and rock n' roll). Somewhere in my psyche I thought if only I could understand that world, then I might have some clue as to why all of a sudden he didn't love me anymore.

Of course it didn't. It just led me into an alcohol and marijuana induced haze of sex with guys I barely knew. And at that time in history—late '60's/early '70's—it was considered cool and hip to be in the drug scene, and "make love not war" as we protested the Vietnam conflict. So my braless, barefoot, long haired "hippie'" appearance was just considered part of the norm for that day. Nothing to be all that concerned about, it seemed like everyone was "tripping out" in those days and getting high all the time, not really present to our lives, not really caring where we were going or what our futures held.

College provided a type of safe haven for my behavior and a place to hide out from my pain. Dorm life only lasted one semester for me. There were too many rules and I kept breaking them. I moved off campus to live with a drug dealer and our days began by getting 'high'.

In my Senior year, I left the university town to do my student teaching. One night the phone rang at this lovely woman's home where I was renting a room, and it was my ex calling! How he found me I'll never know because he died shortly thereafter. During that phone conversation he confessed that when he had said he didn't love me anymore, it wasn't really the Truth. That he had always loved me. Now, at this point I had heard through various grapevines that he was into some pretty heavy stuff, including heroin, but this phone call gave me some closure about the mystery around the breakup. And yet, my vow to never feel that kind of deep pain again had grown very strong, very deep roots inside me.

As I ventured out into the world, I took my closed off heart with me into a 10 year marriage, which of course, failed miserably. I had no idea who I was and some part of me said Yes to this man because I didn't know what else to do next in my life. In the scheme of things, wasn't this what people were supposed to do after they started their careers? I went ahead with the wedding even though I woke up that morning knowing deep inside that it wasn't the right thing.

My divorce and my resignation from my teaching job happened simultaneously and I found myself venturing into the unknown without a clue what I was going to do. As I drove from Iowa to Arizona (the only other place in the U.S. that I knew anyone), I remember saying to my traveling companion that I didn't know what I was going to do with my life, but I knew it would have something to do with helping women <u>know</u> they have a choice about how they live their lives, no matter what their current circumstances.

Soon after relocating, all my years of self-abuse—drinking, drugging, smoking and unconscious emotional eating came to an abrupt halt. The Universe had handed me the check! After a hard workout at the gym, my body literally gave out on me. I struggled to get out of bed, had no energy, my menses ceased again (this time at age 35), and I was so tired that mid morning and mid afternoon naps were the only way I got from sunup to sundown.

It was as if God was saying, "If you want to get up, you need to <u>listen</u> up!" And listen I did. Hard!

After discovering that Western medical professionals deemed me 'in normal ranges' from their testing, even though my body was not functioning as it should in <u>my</u> mind with no periods, and not enough stamina to get through the day, I started looking into alternatives. A friend introduced me to muscle testing and for the next five years, by trial-and-error and with her testing me in health food and homeopathic drug stores, I gradually got well enough to work again.

I had learned a great deal as I was putting my 'Humpty Dumpty' body back together. My study of nutrition, exercise, energy work and spiritual books like "Teachings of the Masters" had put me on an unexpected course of self healing, introspection, and self awareness.

Still with all this knowledge I had had no practical experience in the world of relationships and I fell prey to a romance with a man who was very skilled at drawing forth and using my emotions. He was extraordinarily brilliant at this in his world as a director and screenwriter.

Unfortunately, before my friends could warn me about what they were seeing, I fell deeply and completely into "love', or so I thought. My heart was certainly engaged, but the dynamics of the relationship as I look back on it now, were not those of love but of two people who had come together out of fear. And there I was, giving all my power away to this man, a pattern that was still ingrained in me from my teen years. As you might imagine, this entanglement ended badly, after lots of deceit, and with me weighing in at about 100 lbs. and sleeping very little. It had taken its toll on me emotionally as well as physically and spiritually.

I once again directed my attention inward and delved deeply into spiritual teachings and learned how to work with Ascended Masters, praying fervently for guidance. Soon I found myself in another relationship. This time with a gentle kind hearted man with shared custody of his son. On the surface it appeared that perhaps this would provide some stability for me, a foundation to build on. When we got engaged I envisioned myself as a married woman living in a home with an 'instant family' and that gave me a feeling of safety and security.

Alas, not all was as it appeared. His spiritual path included drugs, which I discovered upon moving in with him. I tried to cope with that for awhile and could feel myself trying to "settle" on some level, turning myself inside out once again to try and make it work. Eventually after a lot of back and forth, gut wrenching breakups, I ended it.

At that point I looked back over my relationship history and realized that I had kept repeating the same patterns over and over again and that my heart just hadn't really been open or fully engaged since my first boyfriend. I was still that wounded, hurt, defiant teenager deep inside. I made the decision to just not go into that arena any more. It always was such a strange tangle of emotions and games and no one, especially me, seemed to know what they were doing in a relationship or how to make them work.

Out on my own again, a chance to be part of a cause came my way and I immersed myself in a project to save our tropical rainforest in Peru. It was great to be part of something bigger than myself and connected with something that would help Mother Earth. My early roots as a farmer's daughter had left a very special place in my heart for the earth and our trees.

It was really easy to get _so_ involved in this project that I could easily ignore any desire to be in an intimate relationship. It was much simpler and seemed so much safer to stay busy with my work than to face my semi-buried pain. My thoughts of helping women, that I had voiced years before, did come through though, loud and clear, and I stepped into a more spiritual world once again, this time determined to ferret out and banish those unhealthy patterns forever.

As I studied, learned, and practiced using energy tools to clear blocks and obstacles, getting to the root of deep emotional patterns and seeing the Gifts that were there, I was invited to take part in a book project. Andrea, the coordinator of the project, explained that it would be a compilation of stories birthed from within us and published in a book to help women heal. Say no more, I was IN! That had been part of my Vision for decades.

At one point in the process of birthing this story, Andrea suggested I 'sit with' it because she had cognized that something was bubbling up for me.

At first I was discouraged thinking, oh shoot, I didn't do this good enough. But I stayed open and within 24 hours, while watching the movie, Dinner with Friends, I had a major ah-ha.

In this movie there is a scene where Greg Kinnear's character is telling his friend what his marriage had been like for him and how he had felt. I suddenly saw my marriage through this character's eyes and felt SO much compassion for my ex-husband along with deep shame for my behavior. I realized how I had been hurting others because I was hurting. I saw how I had attracted men into my life that would assure I could stay inside my own self induced solitary confinement where I would be 'safe' from feeling any of that horrible pain again.

This was a huge turning point for me. After all my years of searching and seeking, this scene in a movie provided a key revelation that opened the door of my solitary confinement.

I felt called to contact my ex-husband and tell him what I had discovered about myself and take responsibility for my part in the marriage not working from a deeper place. The Universe has such a sense of humor.   We ended up speaking on Valentine's Day.

I struggled to choke back tears as I apologized for my constant criticism and belittling during our relationship. I let him know that I realized that hurt people <u>do</u> hurt people and I was deeply ashamed and embarrassed for the pain I had caused him and his family. I let him know it had nothing to do with him, but was born out of my own deeply buried feelings of self-hatred and self-loathing. He was very gracious, saying that we were both very young and that we both had made mistakes. I could feel the mutual love and forgiveness flowing through the phone.

As a result of my having dialed his home phone, his current wife, seeing my number on the caller ID, left me a voicemail. She was very upset and wanted to know why I was calling their house, saying we had been divorced for 20 years and asking just what did I think I was doing contacting them now! I texted my ex and let him know I had received this message and asked him to please reassure her I was not trying to stir up trouble, that I just wanted to take responsibility for my part.

Within an hour, she phoned me again and when I saw her cell number come up I hesitated, wondering what I was going to encounter on the other end. I got into a space of as much love and compassion as I could muster and answered the phone. Within a few seconds of me saying "Hi, how you are you?", sincerely, from my heart, she burst into tears and apologized for the voicemail message. We had a wonderful talk. We had never met before and she told me she had been hearing about me for 20 years and had been afraid to talk to me.

At the end of the conversation she said she was so glad we had the chance to speak and we both agreed that it would be wonderful if we actually met in person one day. It's so amazing that when I was ready, open, and willing, what I needed for my next step in my evolution was right in front of me, and it came through movie dialogue! You just never know where your guidance will come from. It's so interesting what happens when you are totally open, and willing, to receive Source wisdom.

There is an old saying that pain is inevitable but suffering is optional. We always have a choice. What is so ironic to me is that driving cross-country years ago after leaving my marriage and my teaching career, I knew I wanted to help women know they have a choice no matter what their current circumstances. What I didn't realize then was that "**I**" needed to know that, so I could open **my** heart and fully participate in this wonderful gift of life.

I finally get, deep in my cells, that what happened to me as a teenager had nothing to do with my own self worth or love-ability as a person. I was giving love fully from my heart at 16 and it was <u>me</u> who stopped the flow, not my boyfriend. I did this to myself and I was the only one who could turn the faucet back on. This was self-induced pain! Oh my God, all these years it was self-induced pain!

My journey has finally led me back home, home to myself. Learning to love myself is, and continues to be, a major focus in my life as it leads me back to real love.

My heart is expanding every day. I am beginning to open up to people again and healings like the one with my ex husband and his wife are becoming everyday occurrences. At present I'm doing my best to stay in the space of love with my Mom and allow all those years of power struggles to begin to heal. It's not easy, but well worth the effort as more and more love flows between us each day.

My mother's early stage dementia has brought me face to face with the fact once again that we only have so much time on this earth plane and I have made a commitment to myself to live each day to the fullest, with my heart as wide open as I can.

It's time to enjoy my life, instead of hiding out from it.

Maryann Hesse *is continuously evolving, learning, healing, dancing, hiking, doing yoga, reading personal development books, seeking out the best quality dark chocolate, and marveling at nature's beauty and serenity...continuously falling in love with life and the glory of her true self. As an Essence Coach she is passionate about providing a safe place for women to fully express who they are, without judgment, and supporting them in creating lives that are totally fulfilling to them. For more go to:* ***www.about.me/maryannhesse*** *and* ***www.maryannhesse.com.*** *You can contact her at* ***maryann@maryannhesse.com***

Story Nineteen

Pause, Reset, and Hit Play

Fiona Goorman

I breathe and hold   - Whump... Whump… Whump… I slowly release the air out, feeling my chest and my shoulders sink – Whump… Whump… Whump. The blood is pulsing through me and my heart sounds angry and defiant in my ears. Hurt, wounded, angry. Whump… Whump… Whump. My head is under water except for my nose. My bath water is shy of scalding, painful to my skin. It feels real. Eyes closed, to shut out the pain of where I am, what is going on, to shut it all out and focus on my heart beat, my one truth right now, the one thing that is keeping me together, keeping me from exploding into a thousand pieces.

For me there exists this one blissful, suspended moment right before I fully wake up. A suspended moment when I don't remember what is going on, I don't feel any pain or emptiness. Untouched. Unaware. Full. And then it rushes back; ready to bury me in a landslide of emotion. Choke me off, block out the light and push me under. Hurt, crippling hurt. An emptiness inside that pounds in my head, beats at my aching body and burns my stomach. So this is where songs of heartache come from. They are scraped from the bottom of the barrel, sieved out of the puddle of a heart, the love ballad and the solid gold album.

Whump... Whump! The pounding in my head and the pressure becomes too much. Let me out! I sit up in the tub and look down at my lobster legs, my reddened hands, and watch the steam rise off my body. If only the pain and the memories could rise up and drift away forever.

This body will never know his touch again but I feel like he is tattooed all over me. My body. This is my body. When did I give myself to you?! When did I abandon these parts of me? When did I give up on myself? Whose life am I living? Whose life is this anyway? When did I decide that who I am, what I say, how I act, how I feel isn't good enough?

Parts of him are integrated into me, where do I end and he starts? How do I get rid of his imprint on me, in me? He's in my thoughts, my blood. Memories of the outline of his body in my bed, his shape, his smell on my pillow, the feel of his cheek under my lips, the raised vein that runs along his arm, snaking from the corner of his wrist to the soft inside of his elbow.

I have to get rid of this. I don't want it. He doesn't want me anymore. I need to get rid of this, cut it out of me. I start ripping, pulling, tearing myself apart in my desperation to remove him. I don't need you, fuck you, don't call me, don't try to message me, go fuck yourself!

I tear myself apart, I dig into old wounds and I stare into them, running the story over in my mind, repeating, changing, regretting, wondering if it would have been different. Ugly, puffy, blistering memories. I know these places in me and I know the places I've protected, held on to,

194

taken in and formed a shell around; part of me, but still separate. But I haven't hurt like this before. Find the pain, grab it, squeeze it, watch it twitch in my hand. Choke it, throw it against the wall, watch it bleed out on the floor, let it die. The pain will end. Please die.

The interrogation begins again.
What just happened?
Why do I hurt so much?
When did I decide that what I wanted wasn't worth pursuing?
Why am I ok with a one armed hug after a 6-week absence?
Why did I feel I was always accommodating his schedule and getting little in return?
Why was I ok with certain behavior from him that I would have told my best friend was unacceptable if the table was turned?
My confidence, what I believed, what I knew to be true, didn't really exist. Where have I been? How can eight years have passed?

When had I given up on him, not accepted him, made excuses for what was really going on and ignoring the signposts along the way? Ignoring what was chipping away at who I was and who I knew him to be. I don't recognize you anymore. Who are you? And who am I? How did this happen? When did I give up on myself? When did I hit the pause button in my life? And why does part of me no longer care? Ding, ding, ding. When did I stop caring about myself? It is easy to blame him, to make it about him. Realizing how much I was willing to contribute to my own downward spiral, there's the kick in the teeth.

I am at my lowest. I need to feel the bottom because I don't want to feel this way ever again. I don't want to have so much of me, my worth, how I valued and defined myself, to be rocked like this again. To be so entangled with another person that to pull out these bits of him from me, I abandoned the pieces that were mine. Knotted up, wrapped around, meshed together like skin growing into an old band-aid.

Looking back at this time has been uncomfortable; my chest is tightening as I write. But as I look back at one of my lowest points, I know I would not, could not, trade this experience for anything. I needed to get back in touch with myself.

As I write this story, I'm sitting on my back patio on a Sunday morning with a cup of coffee and the sun warming my face. It is June, warm enough to go barefoot, but I'm wearing a long sleeved hoodie. I'm looking at the first iris blooming on the hillside behind my home and the purple tops of the chives bobbing to their own music and I breathe in one of my most favorite smells. Pine pollen. Sun warmed pine pollen. Sweet, sharp, clear and grounding. The smell drifts in but lands like an anchor – reminding me of distinct, pivotal times and places in my life. In a way, this smell defines who I am. When I am searching for who I am, searching for my purpose, questioning my decisions, sun warmed pine pollen reminds me this is exactly where you need to be. Everything is perfect, know this smell and know this is your perfect path.

Kayaking on a lake I smell this, when I moved to northern Saskatchewan for my first full time job, I recall stepping onto thick, springy moss and the connection I felt to the earth, and the smell of pine pollen. I remember walking to my office in northern BC. 15lbs lighter, shadows under my eyes from lack of sleep, a slump in my shoulders. The drag of each step; resistant to any forward movement. Who knew that emptiness could weigh this much? And then, sweet pine pollen. Hey, remember me? It's ok to feel this. Breathe me in, enjoy this moment right now, in the middle of the pain you feel, you are exactly where you need to be. You are in pain and you are alive. There is a reason for this and there is a reason for you.

As I said earlier, I wouldn't trade any of these experiences and I can look back at the devolution of this relationship as being of real service to me. It resulted in a quick move to a different city where I was destined to meet specific people and go through a series of changes, molting and shedding the parts of me I carried to please other people and to open myself to a different paradigm of showing up in my life. I know how to take better care of myself, to meet my needs from a truly authentic place of knowing what I need, not of thinking I know what I need. Being alone allows this, demands this. A patient shifting through the ashes and rubble to find the gems, the hidden core of who I am and to rebuild everything from there.

I can look at the pain I felt during this time and see how I wasn't ready to own up to my part, what I contributed or chose not to contribute, how I acted, the choices I made and how I showed up. So much of my pain came from that part of me that knew I created this. So much of my self worth had been tied up in having him love me, but the cost was I stopped loving part of my self.

I am not writing from a place of having answered my life's big questions. I am writing from a place where I love myself, I've fallen in love with myself again. I have shed some of the burdens of trying to meet other's expectations and I feel a deeper connection to making choices and walking a path that feels good to me. I write, I meditate, I practice yoga and I kayak. I can better recognize when I step into old patterns or recreate situations that don't serve me.

I often set the intention that during my sleep, I will process something that best serves me. Sometimes I dream about him. Even in my dreams he is indifferent. Indifferent about what I say, even about the fact he is in my dream. But more recently, she is there too. His wife. I don't know her name, but it's her. And she is none too impressed about being there, about sharing a space with him and with me. I can attest, that the stink eye comes through in dreams too. One day these dreams will stop, at the perfect time. I welcome that day.

Forgiveness is not separate. There really is no separate forgiveness for him. It is forgiving myself that forgives him.
I forgive myself for wanting love from him.
I forgive myself for changing who I was to better fit into his life.
I forgive myself for abandoning some of my most precious and defining gifts and attributes.
I forgive myself for clinging to certain ideas and throwing away others.
I forgive myself for putting someone else first.

197

I forgive myself for forgetting who I was.
I forgive myself for hitting PAUSE.

If that time in my life can be described as rough and messy butchering, then the last couple of years have been more like a gentle, ongoing practice of daily endoscopy. Non-invasive, innovative, and with a shorter healing time.

I'm so thankful for the self-growth, the learning, the knowledge, and the pain. I needed that pain to force myself to look, to really look. To look at my choices, my decisions, my giving over, my holding back and my rebuilding in an integrated way. Rebuilding in a way what I wasn't aware of before, using new tools. Rebuilding truthfully, honestly, with less judgment, pausing, going at a pace where I can gently remove what doesn't serve me, bless it, and gracefully move on.

More and more I recognize the difference in a mutually beneficial exchange, the benefit of balance. That I can show up, full on ten Fiona, whatever that is for the moment, and people will love it, be indifferent, or deal with it. There is a lot of freedom and peace to be had in being myself.

Having confidence again, in my decisions, in my self worth, my value, my choices. Confidence in knowing what is best for me. Knowing that being alone is best for me right now. Checking in with myself more often, and noticing if I step back into an old pattern, repeating my history.

I can meet my own needs first and truly be of service to me, and then to others. That is ok. This is best. This is for the greatest good. In doing so, I welcome richer experiences with people, I can lose time in a conversation and I can make room in my life for the things I have not even imagined yet.

I'm gentler with myself, I'm gentler with others too, this freedom that I feel in my life right now is something to relish, respect, enjoy and carry forward. My sense of completion about particular areas in my life are soothing to me now and I'm proud of them; like a finished quilt. Over time, some of the stitches may unravel, but when you step back to look, the beauty and pattern of the whole piece overwhelms the detail.

A breeze floats by, cooling my skin. I shiver. Sun warmed pine pollen. Today is a good day to go for a paddle. I breathe in, I smile, I breathe out, close my eyes and open up to my freedom. I feel the rush of my expansion and I thank myself for the courage to hit PLAY again.

Fiona Goorman:

Born and raised in Regina, Saskatchewan, I am the youngest of three daughters from Filipina and Dutch parents who immigrated to Canada in the early 70's. I have an affinity for picking up lyrics. I am in my element belting out songs and dancing during road trips, or any time in the car is fair game really. Right now I am in love with my yoga practice, kayaking, hiking, and meditation. I've had a home with composting worms since 2003. The first sip of my morning coffee is absolute heaven. Add a giant, orange, yolky, basted farm egg, some rye toast, and I have myself a pretty fabulous Sunday morning.

I am grateful for my family, my friends and my adventures while exploring new and old territories. At home, you can often find me on the back patio, enjoying the hillside view, the sunshine and the breeze with Miss Misu, snuggle bum kitty extraordinaire.

Story Twenty

Eight Gifts

Andrea Hylen

This is the story of the loss of my son. *It is* a journey of heartbreak and sadness and *it is* a journey of joy and triumph. When my heart was cracked open and filled with pain, I discovered deeper love and a fuller, richer life.

☼♥☼♥☼♥☼♥☼♥☼♥☼♥☼♥☼♥

In 1993, my son, Cooper died at the age of 19 months after 19 months of surgeries and triumphs. Given the physical challenges he was born with, it was a blessing he was here with us for that long.

     Before I share the story of Cooper, I want to share a few things about the first loss in my life, the death of my baby brother Kenneth who died from SIDS, sudden infant death syndrome. This was my first loss and the beginning of my journey with grief and the power of love.

     It was 1961. I was only 4 years old when Kenneth was born and also when he died at the age of two months. I have vague memories of that day. I remember looking through the bars of his crib and wondering why he wasn't awake yet; I remember being whisked away to the neighbor's house where we played with our friends all day. I remember being offered Hostess cupcakes and Twinkies as an unexpected treat after lunch.

Somewhere in the mix of feelings, I unconsciously began to feel responsible for all of the emotions that were and were not being expressed around me. No one talked about my brother. I also lost my Raggedy Ann Doll. A few months after my brother died, we moved away from a very loving, supportive community in Minnesota for my Dad's job promotion and relocation. These two events of losing both my brother and my doll were mixed up in my 4-year-old mind. It felt like we left them behind. Maybe if I were not a "good girl" I would be left behind, too.

After several more moves, we landed in Texas where we were a part of another community. I remember feeling really safe and loved again.

When I was ten, we took a trip to Massachusetts to attend my great grandfather's funeral. My aunt held me as I sobbed loudly and gasped for breath and gently guided me out of the service. How could I be so sad about the death of my great-grandfather who I had only met a few times? His death and the pain I felt in the room released layers of loss and unexpressed grief. There was no way to understand or express it at my young age. It all came tumbling out of me. The loss of my brother, the loss of moving away from loving communities all tied up in a bundle of pain.

Later in life, when I had children of my own in my thirties, I asked my mother how she had coped after the loss of her son. In a very matter of fact tone, she said, "He was dead. He was gone. That was it." After I got over my initial shock at what appeared to be cold and indifferent, I looked closely to understand the depth of her words.

In 1961, it was not common to talk about the loss of a loved one. My mother had no one to talk to about it. She had to keep it together for her two daughters ages 2 and 4, my sister,

Joanne, and me. Her husband, my father, had a job that required travel and my mother shut the emotion deep within her to cope with life. At the time no one understood how much I was feeling the pain no one was expressing. I could feel my mother's pain even when she told me she was fine.

When I was pregnant with my third child, my only son, I wanted to name him Kenneth after my brother. It felt like a way to connect with my brother, to honor him and to bring him to life. My son became Kenneth Cooper Cox; Kenneth for my brother; Cooper to honor my husband's passion for falconry (Cooper's Hawk) and Cox for my husband's last name. We called him Cooper for short.

I believe with my whole heart that Cooper came to Earth for a short time to teach us and help us to heal. This is the kind of belief that gives me chills when I say it. I can feel the truth in my whole body. He was an angel who came into our lives for a short period of time to teach us about love.

Cooper was my 3rd child. My first two daughters, Mary and Elizabeth, were born into my first marriage that ended in divorce. Cooper and then Hannah were born into my second marriage with my husband Hurley. Cooper died in 1993. Hurley died in 2005.

When I was 7 months pregnant with Cooper, an ultrasound showed an anomaly. Something was wrong with his heart and there was an enlarged lung. No one could predict what would happen in the next two months of growth in my uterus or what would happen when he was born.

On the day of the ultrasound, I went through a wide range of emotions. It started with, "Why me, God? Haven't I been through enough already?" I thought about all of the trauma and loss I had in my life and felt like this had to be a punishment for something.

Returning to the doctor with my husband for more information, I felt calm, focused, determined and armed with questions. I was a warrior mother ready to do whatever I needed to do for my son. I asked the doctor, "What is this? What can we do? How can this be fixed?" There were no definitive answers. All we could do was wait for his birth.

In that state of riding the roller coaster, I went through a series of emotions the rest of the day. Cleansing tears, desperation, and a dash of hope, back to despair, embracing positive words for inner pep talks, and crumbling into misery. The next day I woke up with the inspiration to cross stitch angels. It would give me something to "do" while I waited with him growing for two more months in my womb. The angels would become the place to focus my thoughts and energy. During Cooper's 19-month life, I cross-stitched amazing, sparkly, intricate angel pictures in hospitals, waiting rooms and at home. Each stitch had a prayer. I poured my heart and soul, my wishes, desires and my emotions into the angels. I carried the angels with me like guardians for my son and me. I knew I couldn't control the situation. I couldn't change his physical health. All I could do was find a way to stay connected with my faith, to learn from the opportunities and challenges that were in front of me and believe that with the angels I could support my beautiful son.

The gifts from Cooper began then and are infinite and continue to be a blessing. In this story, I want to share Eight of the Infinite Gifts.

Cooper was born at Johns Hopkins Hospital in Baltimore, Maryland on June 12, 1991, with a team of nurses and doctors ready to receive him and save his life. He lived in intensive care, connected to oxygen, IV fluids and heart monitors until his 1st open-heart surgery. It was after his surgery that the 1st gift appeared.

My husband and I were escorted to "the room." Over the next year and a half, we would learn that this is where the doctors give you bad news. Good news is delivered in the hallway, by the bedside, and in the waiting room. But, when you are asked to step into "the room" it always meant bad news.

The doctors told us that the surgery went well, but Cooper was little and he was weak. They really did not expect him to make it through the night and they wanted us to be prepared.

I took a deep breath and the inner, warrior mother appeared in me. The strength from within knew that there was no time to waste on tears and meltdowns in the "room." It was time for action. I asked if I could see Cooper now. In the short walk down the hallway to his bedside, I made a choice. Sitting by his bed with tears streaming down my face, I held my son's tiny little hand. I looked at the tubes and wires attached to his little body. I told him that I would love him forever and always, no matter what. I told him that if he decided to live, I would be by his side through everything. And I told him that if it were too much to stay here and fight for his life, I would still love him forever. I let him know it was up to him, but I was on his team and I would be here.

Within five minutes, his life signs grew stronger. The beeps and the graphs on the monitors began to rise to healthier, stronger levels. I knew that he had made his decision. He was going to fight for his life.

The 1st gift Cooper gave me was the experience of unconditional love.

As much as I loved my daughters and I loved my husband and I loved my family and friends, I had never had a moment like this. I was so clear that the choice was up to him. I was not going to beg him to live and I was not going to give up. I was going to let him know I was there for him and allow him to make the decision. It was unconditional love, an expression of loving and letting go in a way that I had never experienced before.

During the next few weeks, I was with Cooper at the hospital every day. In order to take him home, I had to learn how to feed him through a tube in his nose and to administer oxygen. As much as I love my children, everyone knows I am not a "nurse type" person. I rented an electric breast pump; a machine I would attach to my breasts to pump the precious nutrients from me into plastic bags we storied in the refrigerator. I learned how to insert a thin plastic tube into my son's nostril, through his esophagus and down into his stomach. This was the path for the breast milk to give him a life force of nutrition. I had to be careful to reach the stomach and avoid puncturing his lungs, listening for the gurgling sounds with a stethoscope. As a warrior mother, I knew that I had to learn how to take care of his medical needs. This was my only choice! Through it all, the staff and my friends reflected that I was a good mother and my commitment and love were the reasons he was still alive.

This was the 2nd gift. Cooper's health challenges and my willingness to do whatever I needed to do to care for him showed me that I was a good mother.

I had been carrying a deep wound in my heart with the break-up of my first marriage. In the crazy divorce, people had judged and tried to prove I was a bad mother. This was never true, but I had heard it so many times the wound was deep. My confidence had been shattered.

Through his numerous surgeries, including a hernia operation and a shunt for hydrocephalus and weekly sessions of physical, speech and occupational therapy and doctor appointments, Cooper survived and grew stronger.

At home, in between the surgeries, we laughed, we danced, read books and sang. He brought joy into our household and helped me to remember the unique gifts I could share with all of my children.

By the time Cooper turned one year old, we had over $10,000 in debt from all of the surgeries, even with expensive, comprehensive Blue Cross/Blue Shield health coverage. One night, I had a dream that we would have a birthday party and ask for cash donations instead of gifts. In the dream, we received $3450 in donations. I took that as an inspiration, organized a party and asked friends and family to celebrate Cooper's birthday with monetary donations instead of presents. We received $3460. This was $10 more than in my dream.

I was able to negotiate with all of the medical institutions and wipe out our debt completely.

The 3rd gift from Cooper was to honor my dreams and my intuition and expect miracles.

When Cooper was in intensive care after the second open-heart surgery, my parents came to visit him in the hospital. Sitting across the bed from each other. I witnessed a conversation between my parents. They talked about the loss of their son, Kenneth. It was the first time they had shared some of their feelings and shared how they had each grieved alone.

This was the 4th gift from Cooper. He gave us the opportunity to heal and talk about the loss of Kenneth, thirty years later.

During the last two weeks of his life, Cooper was in the hospital again. His lung had collapsed. A variety of medical tests were performed on his heart. I called a friend to start a prayer chain. No Facebook in those days, we used the telephone. Within hours, Cooper's health began to decline.

The 5th gift from Cooper was to show me that prayer is powerful. Sometimes it helps us live and sometimes it helps us die. It always works.

Cooper was on all kinds of machines to support him as his health was failing. After a few days, and no clear answers to discover what was wrong, another test was performed. One of his kidneys wasn't "lighting" up after he was injected with a dye. A 4th stage neuro-blastoma cancer was discovered behind his kidney. I suspected at that time that he was telling us he was ready to die, but we couldn't give up yet.

Miraculously, I was also 8 ½ months pregnant at the time with our daughter, Hannah. With Cooper's health challenges, my husband and I had not had a tour of the birth center at Mercy Hospital. On the night we had a tour, across town from Johns Hopkins, Cooper had a cardiac arrest. He was resuscitated and put on life support. It was that night that I knew he was letting us know it was time to go and another little angel would be joining us soon.

Two days before Cooper died, my husband and I sat around a large oval table in a room filled with 20+ doctors, nurses and hospital staff. We asked for each person's opinion.

My husband asked one of the doctors, "If it were your son, what would you do?" He said, "I think I would say, how many hits does a kid need to take?" It was in that room, in that moment, that we decided to turn off the life support. In the next 24 hours, we let friends and family know that we would be turning off the life support the next day. My husband and I talked with each other to see what we each needed to do before letting our little boy go.

On the last day of Cooper's life, on Jan 15, 1993, Hurley sat in a rocking chair with Cooper on his lap. With my belly full with our 4th child, I sat on the floor with my head resting on them both. We signaled the doctor with a nod of our heads that it was time to turn off the life support. When I saw Cooper take his last breath, I felt a solid hug from behind. I turned my head to acknowledge my sister-in-law, Patty, and to thank her for being there with us. The hug was so strong I felt it had to be her. But, when I looked, she was still on the other side of the bed. There was no one behind me. I knew in that moment it was Cooper giving me a hug.

The 6th gift was the hug and knowing that life goes on. It was a moment when my faith turned into life experience. The 7th gift came two weeks later when Hannah was born. Cooper died on Jan 15, the memorial service was on Jan 23, and on Jan 30, Hannah was born.

I feel that the gift was presented to me from Cooper and Hannah. Through the process of grieving the loss of my son and loving and caring for my new baby, I learned that I could feel grief in one moment and joy in the next. I learned that as human beings we are capable even in the darkest of times of feeling everything. I learned that the ability to go into the deep core of pain and find the light is where we can learn to live from a fuller and richer place. It is like entering into a deep, dark cave and being willing to turn on the flashlight to see what is really there. It is the willingness to feel everything.

And the 8th gift was to open my eyes to live and appreciate the time we have together.

During Cooper's life we laughed, we danced, we sang and appreciated the time we had. He taught me to connect with something or someone you are in love with every day; even in intensive care there are beautiful moments. He taught me to live today without waiting for a perfect picture to appear and to…

Live

    A

        Life

            Worth

                Celebrating

Andrea Hylen *believes in the power of a woman's voice to usher in a new world. She is the founder of Heal My Voice, a Minister of Spiritual Peacemaking, a Life Energy Coach and co-author of Conscious Choices: An Evolutionary Woman's Guide to Life. Andrea has discovered her unique gifts while parenting three daughters and learning to celebrate life after the deaths of her brother, son and husband. She currently lives in Los Angeles following the inspiration to collaborate with women in community and to travel around the world speaking and leading workshops. Her passion is connecting women to support each other in the full expression of who they are. To connect with Andrea and learn about current projects go to: www.andreahylen.com and www.healmyvoice.org.*

Story Twenty-One

My Boring Old Story

Marie Ek Lipanovska

I am pretty tired of my history, tired of telling the same thing
over and over again. I was born in a family where my father
was an alcoholic. My parents divorced when I was six. So he
moved out. Growing up in this dysfunctional environment
has shaped my entire life, in all areas. And it has been
devastating to my relationships.

Not having a father's love has made me search for that
love in every man I have ever known. Only one could live up
to that standard. It was a teacher at school when I was
between ten and thirteen years old. He gave me hope. I met a
man with a stronger energy than mine. They do exist.
I have felt abandoned all my life. It felt like no one ever
listened to me. I longed to be the chosen one, someone's
princess. But no, life has not made me a princess. Instead, I
became a warrior. A warrior for justice. I became a warrior

and a voice for those who couldn't speak up and stand up for themselves. My father stole that arena from me to perform and be seen. He owned the show. He played the same show over and over again. The show about the victim. His terrible childhood. His father. A monolog with a never-ending show of self-pity and egoism. My father was a child, so that role was already taken. I became the father he didn't want to play. And I took on the responsibility to create a calm place.

I have few memories from my younger childhood. But the worst period was when I was a teenager. My mother allowed him to come and visit whenever he wanted, as long as he was sober. But that didn't matter to me, since he was allowed to drink in our home anyway. I know my mum did the best she could. I have always felt her love. But her lack of power and responsibility caused me a lot of pain. She allowed him to drink in our home and she sometimes drank together with him. I never felt she had a problem with alcohol, but I hated to see her lower herself to his level. In my eyes she lost her dignity. I looked at him with pity. I saw a child that was lost in a bottle. But I saw my mother lose the glory I had put on her. And she never got it back. Somewhere in that age I lost some of my respect for her. I couldn't trust her. I became the parent for both of them. And she handed the problem over to me, literally. I was the father, the mother and the child at the same time. I can understand that she wanted him to visit us. I am grateful for that. She kept the door open to him. But she also opened up the door for something else.

I saw no affection between a man and a woman. I had no one to learn from. They as parents couldn't show me how love worked in a relationship. They both chose to live a single life after the divorce. I don't blame them for that. But, there were no models for healthy, love relationships.

My mother gave me space to be who I was. All emotions were allowed. There was a lot of hugging between the two of us. I know she really loved me and she was proud of me. She still is. But I became the parent in our relationship too. Our roles shifted. When my father was drunk and she couldn't handle him, she went to bed. I had to throw him out. I literally pushed that drunken body filled with self-pity out of our apartment. And I hated him when he looked me in the eyes and said, "How can you do this to your own father?" I don't remember if I replied. I just shoved him out and threw his shoes after him before I closed the door. But inside I cried. I hated the sound of clinking bottles in the plastic bag from the liqueur store. I hated the smell of an old man, his empty eyes and the body that had no pride and no power. The bottles meant trouble for me. His presence meant trouble. No rest, but hours of work. Soon two adults would turn into selfish children. My four-year-old brother would hide in his room. I had to work. I was the youngest, doing the dirty job.

I remember one episode very well. It was late autumn or early wintertime. My father had no apartment at that time. I knew he had nowhere to go when he left our home that evening. My mother refused to let him stay over night. I live in Sweden. It was cold outside! I had mixed feelings. I felt sorry for him. He was my father and I was scared he would die from the cold. From the window, I saw him walk out of the street door six floors down. He headed to the shed in the yard where everybody in the building stored their bikes and we kids sometimes hanged out. He slept that night in that shed. I didn't know what I felt would be the worst scenario. If he died out in the cold or some of my friends saw him sleeping in the shed.

I was mad about the situation. It was so wrong. No one did anything. My father didn't seek any help. My mother didn't do anything to change the situation we all had to put up with. We kids didn't get any help. I didn't know what to do. I only knew something needed to be done, but nothing happened. It all just went on.

I don't know how to be in a relationship with men. I had no adults, no teachers, only bad examples. I am still a student who wants to learn how to keep a relationship going. I have tried giving all of me. I became too much. Too much love. Too much sadness, way too much joy and too much of everything. The men got scared of all the emotions. So I tried to close down and give little. That worked for seventeen years in my marriage. I have three healthy, beautiful children. I left the marriage with a lot of money when we sold our house in the divorce. I was a great mum, but a terrible wife sometimes.

A control freak. It took me seven years to trust him. I was happy in one moment sad in the next. Patient in one moment and like Hitler in the next. Unbalanced. I was the caretaker with all the responsibility, the coordinator, and we lived by my rules. With that role, my femininity slowly died along with my vulnerability and passion. We stopped making love. Weeks without sex became months and turned into half a year. My soul became silent. I stopped talking. I felt I was dying. He couldn't do anything. I closed down all my emotions and my body. Finally I had to leave or I would have died. We are good friends today. We handled the divorce great.

And in that space of being alone, no longer a full time mother, I had to look at myself deeply. I awakened to life again. I started my own business. I found self-love, dignity, peace of mind, my inner voice, my calling. God became my father. And then heaven entered my life. I met my Soul Mate. I lived in Paradise for a while. I blossomed. We connected in mind, body and soul. We had heavenly sex and became one spirit. But I was the adult child of an alcoholic and he was a sober alcoholic. We were doomed to fail. I didn't have the tools for a successful love relationship. Neither did he. All we had was our divine love and our history. And the history had more power and more years to lean on. We had no tools for handling the fear that came with that amount of love we both felt.

I could write a whole book for everything I am grateful for that has come out of my childhood, my marriage and my soul mate relationship. I treasure the gifts. I honor them. They have made me who I am. And I am proud of myself. But I am tired beyond infinity. I don't want to be a warrior any longer. I want to be the princess and grow up to be the queen that rules the kingdom with love and compassion. I want to be healed and to let go of this boring history of mine. I want to live, not only survive. I want pleasure and ease. I want love, love and even more love. 24-7.

When I look back I see that I have been on a long journey. Travelling from innocence to guilt and back to innocence. From Love, to fear and back to the Land of Love again. I haven't arrived in a new place. I am back where it all started 44 years ago. I have undressed myself from the guilt, the shame, the fear, the pain and suffering, the loneliness, the separation, the wounds, the not perfect, the blame, the judgment and all the other emotions that life has dressed me in. I have been a victim and a martyr.

I have lost my Soul Mate and all the money. I put the money into love. How did that pay off? That could mean that an open heart and believing in the power of love is a path to poverty on every level in life. But I refuse to believe that. An open heart and sharing that love by giving and receiving has to be the formula for prosperity. Otherwise I see no point in living or surviving. I see that I have learned things along the way that have brought me back to the Land of Love and Truth. Or should I say, I have unlearned what life taught me that life was all about. And I see now that after the divorce I put the money, the effort, the time and the love into intensive care for myself. I, as the adult, finally put the light on my boring old history and gave my inner child the attention she needed to heal her wounds.

I want love to win the war even if I lost some battles along the way. I want to sit on my throne smiling and knowing I have overcome my history by keeping my heart open for love. We are all love. We are all one. When I love you. I love myself. When you love me. You love yourself. I am Love. You are Love...Always.

Marie Ek Lipanovska *is a woman with passion and power, the founder of Open Heart Business and Community. Marie believes in empowering women to become liberated authentic leaders by teaching them to listen and speak from an open heart, combined with finding a financial independency so they can serve their soul mission. She is a passionate writer, speaker and an Essence Coach, living her life with presence and pleasure. Marie turns to the world from her home in Malmoe, Sweden. Her favorite words are love, joy, courage, faith and liberation and she finds it inspiring to write sensual short stories.*

In September 2012 Marie will extend Andrea Hylen's mission by managing the first edition of Heal My Voice Sweden.
www.ohbac.se *and* ***www.healmyvoicesweden.se***
www.marie-eklipanovska.se

Story Twenty-Two

Betrayal

Karen Porter

Sitting at the registration table waiting for stragglers, latecomers to the conference where I was volunteering, I received the call that my aunt was in the hospital.
My Aunt Pearl had told no one.

Four years prior, she first noticed a lump in her scalp. She decided not to seek any medical treatment. She sold her home and bought an apartment in a continuous care facility, the reason, she said, was that having no children she did not want to be a burden on her extended family in the future. She called the shots. She was used to that. Working nearly 50 years at the same job, an administrator of a high school, where everyone openly acknowledged that she ran the school, my very proper, white-gloved Aunt Pearl ruled with an iron fist. On the board of her church, a docent at a nearby historical

217

site, and active in her community, she appeared to be in charge and in total control of all areas of her life.

Her biggest regret, her life's flaw, was her choice of a husband. It was my first therapist, a psychiatrist, who labeled him after hearing the stories of his exploits, as polymorph perverse. He would fuck anything, women, men, children, dogs. Control was his game and his primary target was his wife. The one time Aunt Pearl learned of an infidelity and was told about his 'touching' my older sister, he made it clear that if she divorced him, she would be ruined. He would take the house, everything she had worked for, and ruin her reputation. The early 1960s was not a welcoming time for divorcees. While knowledge of an affair may have been whispered about, one did not speak of such things as child sexual abuse. In trying to determine whether I had been abused, I remember my father yelling at me, demanding to know if he had ever 'hurt' me. I was young, probably six years old, and to that point, what he had done to me and had me do to him never 'hurt', so I said no. The uncle had known to start grooming me and abusing me much younger than he tried with my sister.

The abuse began the summer I turned three years old. I can see the difference in old photos. The beautiful, smiling, happy baby girl posing in a new spring outfit, holding a full Easter basket was so different from the sullen girl, slumped, head resting on forearm on the back of her chair, not even looking at the camera at Thanksgiving dinner.
"Good girls don't tell. Emily was a bad girl. She told. Good girls don't tell."

I heard that every time. Of course, my not knowing that 'hurt' meant 'touch', my not telling emboldened him and escalated the abuse. It continued until I was 11. The last instance was on the day I had my first period. It was brutal, but that had happened many times before. What made it different was that afterward, in the kitchen, he reached into the drawer where they kept their knives, saying that he would always have "a piece" of me. That scared me. I ran back to my grandparents' house next door, went to the bathroom and saw that I was bleeding. I thought he had somehow snuck a knife into the bedroom and carved that 'piece' from me.

I disclosed the abuse to my family about ten years later. After a serious car accident, post traumatic stress kicked in and I started therapy. About a year into therapy, one morning I awoke to see his car parked in our driveway. Hearing his dogs barking, I knew he had brought the dogs down to 'run' them. They barked while chasing and maybe catching and killing rabbits. What else would he do? I checked that the door was locked and I stayed in bed, nauseous, shaking until he left. I had to be safe in my own home. With my sister's support, I told my parents, aunt and grandmother. Aunt Pearl was devastated. My grandmother thought she had 'handled' the matter after my sister was abused by confronting him and telling him never to do that again. She believed that was the end of it. My father made it clear that he was never to come to our house or step foot on our property again. My aunt, again, chose him.

She chose to stay married to him and was clear that if he was not welcome in our house, she would not come either. While she did visit during the year, holidays remained a problem until he died.

My mother cried every Thanksgiving and Christmas. Thanksgiving was her holiday to have the whole family to dinner and Christmas day had always started for us at home, then my Grandmother had dinner and we would spend the rest of the day at my aunt's house. My mother had everyone for dinner the day after Christmas. One Thanksgiving, I had avoided sitting at the same dinner table with him by being 'sick' and staying in bed that day. I cried and plugged my ears trying not to hear his voice. I cried into my pillow so as not to scream, "Get out. I hate you. Stay away." The Thanksgiving before I disclosed, I spent the day at the movies, to avoid having to deal with his presence. Easters were different. My parents and Aunt Pearl began to travel, taking trips so as not to be home for that holiday. It was fine to go on a vacation without the child-fucking husband, just not to attend a family dinner without him.

She stayed married to him. She never disguised her contempt for him or her displeasure with marriage. He died of cancer four or five years after I disclosed the abuse. My grandmother found him. He was naked and had locked himself and the dog in the bathroom.

After his death, family celebrations resumed, and the only time 'he' was ever mentioned was when I would bring up the fact of the abuse, or something I was dealing with in therapy. With the exception of my dad, my family's reaction would be some form of, "We thought you were over that." I am continuing to learn what it takes to 'get over it'. It is like cruising down the road and hitting a deep pothole. You don't see it coming and it is shocking. It jars the body with a bone deep jolt of reality, sudden and painful.

During the year of intense energy work and training, while both reading others' energies and having my own energy read and issues identified, aspects of my wounding came up, presenting opportunities for healing. Three months before the phone call, during a reading, I saw a step, an action I needed to physically take to heal. I knew I had to lay flowers on his grave.

Before that, visits to his grave were for confrontation and anger release. Once, I brought an herbicide in a squirt bottle and wrote "child molester" across the grave. I fantasized soaking his grave with lighter fluid and setting it ablaze. During that reading, in that meditative moment, I clearly saw and absolutely knew that I had to honor his path. So after a stop at Safeway, because they did not have to be expensive flowers, I drove to the cemetery, growing more nauseous by the minute. Feeling breathless, a bit dizzy and ready to vomit, I stood at his grave. I cannot remember exactly what I said but the intent was to not condone his actions, but to honor our soul level agreements and that what happened during my childhood provided lessons, learning and growth. I laid the flowers on the grave and left.

The release was huge. I felt an enormous energetic shift in my life. I thought I was finished. Then Aunt Pearl's process began. When we returned from being away, Aunt Pearl was still in the hospital, waiting for test results. Just having the tests drained her of strength. She weighed less than one hundred pounds and continued to lose weight. Seeing her without her wig, basically bald with a bandaged, egg sized lump on her scalp was a shock. The only person to have known anything was her hairdresser. Doctors could not believe that her personal doctor did not know. "There was no reason for him to see me without my wig," was her answer.

 One of the questions patients are routinely asked is if information can be shared with people outside the immediate family. "Yes," was her reply. "If anyone cares enough to ask, they can know everything." I made calls for her to friends from work, the community and her church. When her pastor asked if it was fine to share the information with the other church members, I repeated what Aunt Pearl had said. "Care enough to ask about her?" Pastor Lorrie demanded, "Doesn't she know how much she is loved?"

Aunt Pearl chose to leave the hospital and wait for test results and begin physical therapy in the nursing wing of the facility where she lived. Two weeks after the first seizure, Aunt Pearl was sent back to the hospital because she exhibited symptoms of having had a stroke. She had lost use of one side of her body, her mouth sagged, she drooled and her eye was sunken back into her skull. In the emergency room, it looked very possible that she might not survive the night. She told us she loved us and that she was at peace and ready to go with God.

After it was determined there had been no stroke and she began to show some progress in regaining the strength on the affected side, she returned to the nursing wing. She gained some function and was able to do bits and pieces of physical therapy. She wanted to be able to go back to her apartment but thought the best she would manage was the middle step of assisted living. She wanted to make decisions about her belongings so I proposed the idea of making Christmas gift bags for family and friends.

I took her to the apartment where she directed me from her wheelchair as to who was to be given what. The first afternoon she lasted for about an hour and a half before needing to return to her room. On the second trip, we went through her jewelry and she chose pieces for each of us. Whether it was a strand of pearls, a ring or a pin, everyone got 'pearls from Pearl' in addition to the items she matched to each recipient. On that afternoon, it was only forty-five minutes before she was exhausted and needed to sleep. Her tumor was inoperable; its tentacles had grown through her brain and beyond. It was not cancerous. The doctor speculated that she had probably had it for decades. The only option for treatment was radiation that might shrink the tumor but could also initially make it worse and might have no effect except to tax the little strength she had. She decided not to have treatment.

I was with her when she had another seizure. The doctor increased the anti-seizure medicine and when I asked him about calling in hospice, he totally supported that step. My brother, Dan, his wife, Peg, my husband David and I talked with Aunt Pearl that evening. I did all the talking, despite my swatting my brother's leg to get him to help. Aunt Pearl was at peace with dying.

She dictated letters to the family and to friends. She quite enjoyed having a secretary and had me write that in many of the letters. The first day went well. During the second day of dictation, she could not think of what she wanted to say beyond a thought or two. She just did not know. We saw her lose ground every day. What she could do one day she would be unable to do the next. The first ability she lost was walking. She could not get her feet to move. Then it was standing. She even slid out of a chair one afternoon. Her upper body function diminished until she could barely move her arms. She lost control of her bladder and bowels.

This little iron lady became totally dependent and she did not like it one bit. But she did learn to ask for help and she was very appreciative of the good care she received. She also lost any ability or desire to self-censor. When she was told, "I'll be right back," her answer was, "You lie."

I called her friends, called extended family. She had visitors every day. Her new family, residents of the facility, visited her often. Of course she showed them a possible future so some did not return. Her dearest wish was to see a close friend who lived several hours away. The day Dottie came, we took her back to her apartment, with all the Christmas bags lined up, filling a third of her living room floor. It took Aunt Pearl three days to recover from the exhaustion of the visit. That was the last time she left her room.

Cards covered every bulletin board. I made laminated days of the week signs so Aunt Pearl would know what day it was once she could no longer remember. Flowers lined the deep windowsills and crowded the top of her bureau. Many visitors continued to come daily. My father was taken to spend time with her several times. It meant so much. "Norbert doesn't visit anybody." Aunt Pearl allowed herself to feel the love of others. She learned to accept care with grace. Hospice provided medication to manage the pain of her nerve endings overacting. It hurt her to be touched, moved, and repositioned. Her breathing and heart rate remained strong and steady and there was no way to determine how long she would remain in that state.

As she started to talk more of seeing her mother and father and sister, my mother, I had an energy reading and in it I specifically asked Source if there was something I could do to help Aunt Pearl transition. The answer that came was that she needed to hear that I did not blame her for what her husband had done. I even asked if it could be done on an energetic, spirit level. The answer was, "No. She needs to hear the words."

A few hours later, I was on a call with some of the women in this book project, and through sobs, asked for their support, sharing with them what needed to be done. After the call, I went to see and talk with Aunt Pearl. She had begun sleeping more each day and I woke her, saying that there was something I needed to tell her.

I told that I loved her, and that I did not hold her at all responsible or to blame for what he had done. She replied, "Good. I hoped you felt that way." Then I lied. I told her my mother had come to me in a dream (which she does at times) and told me, "You need to say it. She needs to hear the words."

Aunt Pearl wagged her finger at me, and said emphatically, "She was right."

Aunt Pearl passed away 36 hours later. From the first seizure, the first major symptom of the tumor's effect, to her death, it had been nine weeks.

I was left feeling satisfied that I had told her what I did and unsettled that I did not fully believe everything I said. What I did, I did for her. I still needed to do things for ME. The few items she kept of his, a ring, a watch and an old work identification badge were placed in her coffin, out of sight. As some of her possessions came into my house, a few could not stay. Of the set of dining room chairs, 'his' chair was donated. Items were distributed, family members claimed many things and the rest was donated or given to the facility's resale shop. Still, I felt incomplete. The thank you notes I wrote, the Christmas cards I sent to her friends who had not been called or had not come to the funeral home, those things I was doing for her. And that was fine. It was not until just this week, five months after her passing, that I felt a completion.

In clearing out our basement, I unearthed dozens of photo albums. I decided to cull through them, making an abbreviated album for us and albums for each of our sons. I found albums from my mother and knew there were others at my dad's house. In retrieving them, I found albums that were my grandmother's with amazing old photos of ancestors I had never seen. There were also photos of him.

I did some ritual burning of his image, which felt very good, and I also saw a very young me and a younger Aunt Pearl. I saw the 30 and 40-year-old Pearl in a time that would not support her. I revisited the age of secrecy and unmentionable acts. I saw the belief of 'you made your bed', of being stuck and not seeing viable options. While I had said those things and known them in my head, I accessed an understanding of the depth and reality in my heart.
I honor the role each of us took on as part of our life's journey. I am grateful for the healing and learning. I accept and welcome that this is a process and I open to the continued unfolding. And for now, I am complete.

Afterword

This is the story of my process of dealing with betrayal issues. I in no way want to present that I was alone in caring for my Aunt in her final weeks. I wish to acknowledge and honor my brother, husband and especially my sister-in-law, Peggy. She was an angel. For several weeks, she came every night after work and spent the evening with Aunt Pearl, helping her get ready for bed until it became unsafe for her to assist her and then she continued to come, taking and returning laundry, always talkative and cheerful. After those first few weeks, we alternated nights to give her some breaks since Peg really put her own life on hold to be there for Aunt Pearl. During the final days, we were all present each day.

Karen Porter *is a founder of Essence Coaches and serves on the Board of Heal My Voice. Karen is a contributing author to* <u>Fearless Voices: True Stories by Courageous Women</u> *and she co-authored* <u>Conscious Choices, An Evolutionary Woman's Guide to Life</u>.

Karen is an ordained Minister of Spiritual Peacemaking and leads healing meditations incorporating Tibetan Singing Bowls. In 1991, Karen was the first parent to travel to the USSR to adopt and seeing the conditions in her sons' orphanages began relief work and co-founded Children in Common. Karen's academic degree was earned at the College of Notre Dame.

You can contact Karen through ***www.essencecoaches.com***, ***karen@essencecoaches.com***, ***https://www.facebook.com/experiencethepower*** *or listen in on 'Mama Porter Tells It Like It Is' at* ***http://www.blogtalkradio.com/healmyvoice***

Story Twenty-three

A Short Story of My Long Life

Teri Keating

I was the third child of the first litter. My parents divorced and remarried into new families when I was an infant. My challenge of being a caretaker began early. I am from the baby boomer age, and somehow, I had a deep ingrained program to define myself through marriage, parenting and domestication. I would put a rock under my Barbie's dresses to pretend she was pregnant. Mr. and Mrs. had a lovely home, a nice car in the garage and a few beautiful children. My obsession with this picture haunted me for years to come. This was my first real hard lesson I learned.

At sixteen, I had another dream. I wanted to be in front of a camera, both still and film. My mom used to dress my sister and me alike calling us her, "beautiful little girls". I remember when she would take my little head with both her hands and say, "just look at this face". Could this be the reason I had such a burning desire to get comfortable with the lens of celluloid? I soon became a model and a commercial actress, traveling the world and back again. Did I mention, it paid me handsomely? Someone once told me back then, "that luck is when opportunity meets preparation". Those words have stuck with me ever since and left an indelible mark as I walked through the thick and thin of my journey this lifetime.

It certainly wasn't always a bed of roses. My life definitely had its way of throwing me curve balls when I wasn't looking. The second real hard lesson was learning the art of rejection. I wonder if I ever will master it totally. Although, for every "no" I've heard, whether from my parents, teachers, a sibling or a spouse...I always felt I was that much closer to a big fat, YES! I think choosing a career where getting right with rejection has ultimately been a gift. I seem to welcome it like an old friend who comes every now and then to remind me of self worth at my very core!

By the time I turned twenty-nine, I looked down at that biological clock and wondered to myself, "where IS my marriage, my baby (s), our home with the white picket fence and a station wagon"? I'd better get on it, fast. And fast I did. I met, married and conceived my only child in a mere three months. In the two and a half years that followed, I was a single mother, joining the big D club, fighting a heinous custody battle that, ironically, lasted longer than the marriage. A divorce that cost us both a ridiculous amount of money and the loss of that dream of my perfect little family. This was the third real hard lesson learned.

Our son was like raising ten kids! He was a very bright and different child who has been my greatest challenge AND my biggest gift, at the same time. I was the mother who was called almost weekly throughout his schooling with yet another situation he was disciplined for. His teacher's suggested, early on, testing him for ADHD, Attention Deficit Hyperactivity Disorder. I thought to myself, just the length of that medical term gave me a rebellious edge to prove him wrongly diagnosed. I was never one for labels, not on my clothes and certainly not on my beautiful baby boy. I stopped working, moved to the small town of Taos, NM, and put my full attention to his remedial needs. I remember the day I slid down the wall in absolute defeat, screaming at the top of my very tired lungs, begging for help from anywhere. This was right around the same time our world change forever. 9/11 happened and life was looking pretty bleak to me as I questioned every choice I made. My plea was answered in the form of a boarding school for dyslexic boys in Putney, VT. I took out a hundred and fifty thousand dollars in student loans. I know I could not have done that in today's economy. It turned out to be one of the best decisions I ever made yet unfortunately without his father's help. In three years time, our son graduated with the Headmaster's Cup! An award not given out every year, but because of his incredible growth from start to finish, he happily received what he calls, his very own Oscar! There wasn't a dry eye in the house at the graduation ceremonies, including that of his father's. This was the fourth real hard lesson I learned and one I know will never end when it comes to being the best parent I can be. It was now time to get back to my career.

But what was my career, I asked myself? I could feel I was getting to the point where promoting products I didn't use or felt were unethically made was playing hard on my Soul. There had to be another way to flourish. Besides, I could feel the world at large changing in a big way. I could feel something on the horizon getting ready to blow the lid of humanity's ugly facade. Mine especially! I always felt different my whole life and pretty much kept myself on the outside of the in crowd. I knew deep down inside I came here for something more than what I was living. But where to start looking was my constant unanswered question. I had dabbled in various mystery schools and walked on a hot bed of coals. I often dared myself to jump off high places. One time down in lower New Mexico, I climbed up to what looked like a medium size cliff. By the time I arrived at the top, I could see there was no turning back and had to jump forward. By mid flight, I felt this moment of absolute abandonment of my physical body. This must be what death feels like, I thought.

Actually, I did feel like I was going to die, at one point. I don't remember hitting the water but I did finally come up for air to realize I was still here. This was my fifth real hard lesson learned. We all are going back to where we once came eventually.

That was ten years ago, and I've been asking myself that same question every day. When the opportunity came to write a story for this book...I struggled for nine months with what is it that I truly wanted to say. What IS my message? Is it an ongoing question that, with the rest of humanity, is ultimately unanswerable? I feel like I've been going through a portal of some kind. A journey of the sum of every choice I've made to date. My best friend crossed over exactly a year ago today, June 30, 2011. She was my touchstone and a mentor for me. Especially, when it came to listening and supporting my dilemmas throughout our long friendship. She left her cancer-ridden body in just two short months. I honor her and feel her Spirit with me every day since. This was a turning point for me. I am truly heading in a direction where I can feel my most raw and authentic self-emerging.

My relationship with my family of this lifetime feels strange yet perfectly imperfect. I love each one of them equally for the journey we've taken together and still wonder often where I fit in. My correspondence with the man I had my baby with is nothing but silent. My parents are elderly and watching them age reminds me of my own mortality. My son is twenty-two years old and struggles with the normal problems of becoming a man in our ever-changing world. I feel so much compassion for him and all of our youth. It is becoming more and more apparent that we are in very different times. A new dimension of being, with endless possibilities!

I have always resonated with the notion that I was floating about out there in my spirit body when I made a conscious choice to come here and learn the lessons I have learned. I get such an eerie feeling, yet oddly comforting, when I meet someone and it seems like we met before. A kind of remembrance of several lifetimes gone by. I still beg the question, "What is the purpose beyond this life I have chosen"? I know I am here for a reason and I feel that reason is to reflect back light onto everyone I see. The Beatles said it perfectly..."I am me and you are he and we are all together." Each of us so individually different in a very familiar way.

Today, I know, now, why it took me to be the very last one to read my story in this amazing group of women. I kept feeling there was still something I needed to say but what was it? Each day, as each woman read her story, and put her words in the sacred circle for this book...I would go out and sit in my car and listen undisturbed by any distractions. It was as if each woman's story was written just for me! I went on a journey back into my life with every word that was spoken. I could relate on such a deep level with her pain and ultimate resolve with finding her Empowered Voice. As I sat silently looking out at the trees, the sky and the colors in front of me...a feeling of how fleeting our lives can seem when we are still living in, as one story is called, "My Boring Old Story."

Over the course of my spiritual journey, I have collected writings and written some of them myself. These are the words I have said every day <u>at 11:11 am</u> for the past twenty plus years and hoped to live by as I ingrained them into my psyche.

I start out by facing East and with my arms reaching toward the Central Sun, I say, "O Divine Spirit, thank you for pouring thy radiance through my mind and body. And seeing that thy wisdom direct always in everything I do today and every day thereafter". I state the month, day and year. Then I turn to the South, and say, "I am fully present in a place of the mystery, wherein my intention, energy, space and consciousness becomes one. Into this clearing of pure energy, I release my fears and awaken to my experience of true peace and serenity. I embrace the sweetness of Life without reservation or limitation. This or something better has manifested for me now. And so it is!

My arms are still reaching upward toward Divine Source as I envision Golden Light pouring down through me, in me and beyond me. I then turned to the West and say, "It is my Divine intention, energy, space and consciousness, that I have blessed and released the little girl with fantasies and fairytales, and I have come out into the Light where I own and accept my true worth and stature in all the healed worlds. And only that which is from the Great Infinite Intelligence of every Cosmos, Universe, Infiniverse, Galaxy and Milky Way. With the Angelic realm of the Angels, Arch Angels and whole Company of Heaven by my side. And last but certainly not least, my beautiful Spiritual guides.

The prayers to the North are my favorite. In my altered state, I feel like I'm coming in for a landing, touching down softly into the day ahead of me. I say, "It is my divine energy, space and consciousness that this day, (I stated the month, day and year again), is met with ever lasting health, joy, peace, serenity, tranquility, surrender, divine order, divine justice, divine communication and divinity in every aspect of my life. Divine love with myself, my Higher Self, my Highest Self, my son, my life partner (who by the way, I can feel is manifesting before my very eyes), my mother, my father's, my sister's, my brother's, my friend's, my foes, my city, my country, my whole world out to the furtherest Intergalactic gateway from the heart of Mother Earth and beyonds and back again!

It may sound like a lot of mumbo jumbo but it has served me in a way where I really can feel it missing on the days I don't do it.

The last direction is to the East again where I say, "Spiritual guides, Angels and Arch Angels and the Great Grandfather Creator of the Central Sun...Thank you for showing me what it is I am to learn, teach, give and receive. All in the name of your Love, Light and healing for all humanity. Yesterday is history, tomorrow's a mystery, today is all we have. I go forth through this day, (stating the date/year again), with Peace in my Heart, Love in my Eyes and Laughter on my Tongue. I let go of my oars and float down my river of abundance towards the door in which I effortlessly open and step inside. It is my greatest intention here, to be following my bliss, living in my joy and aligning with all the good that awaits me. It is my greatest intention to be in the company of creative ideals, visions, integrity, and dignity making an endless fruitful income and recycling it to where I am serving humanity from the place of my divine birthright of abundance.

And so it is!

☼♥☼♥☼♥☼♥☼♥☼♥☼♥☼♥☼♥☼♥

As I approach my mid fifties, I continue down my path of hard lessons learned and I am sure a few more to come. My burning question that has so eluded me my entire life just may have been answered now! The answer I can find in each day, in every present moment, the choice to serve myself so I can serve humanity with the message I came here to give. My message is to simply love and be love, in a state of grace and deep connection with every breathing creature on the planet. I can now hear, feel and welcome, with all my being, that big fat, YES!

Teri Keating began her career in the fashion industry in 1976. After traveling extensively both nationally and internationally, she settled in Los Angeles in 1979-2008. There she expanded to film/television and advertising commercials for several companies like AT&T, Kellogg's, Sears, Visa and hundreds more. She now lives in Santa Fe, New Mexico working in the health, wellness and personal growth fields in between her modeling/acting assignments. Teri is motivated by birthing in the New Cosmos.

Teri can be reached at rubylite1@me.com

Story Twenty-four
A Poem:

Open Space

Anita (Ani) Pathik Law

A note from the editor: As Ani was connecting with Source and writing a blessing for the book, a poem appeared. She gifted it to include in the book, if it would serve and bless.

We think it does!

A beautiful gift!

Enjoy and feel the Open Space.

OPEN SPACE

Open the space
For love divine
To dance over your edges
transforming reason into rhyme

Breathe in the majesty
Of both joy and despair
Breath in the light
That lingers invisible in the air

See through new eyes
Tuned to beauty and perfection
Embrace all of your shadows
And they'll fade in their projections

Love in the ways
You never dreamed you could
Dare to dare the dreams
Your creator said you would

Be all you've thought
You'd never get to be
Unimpeded by doubt or expectation
Lays your path to free

Awaken in this instant
To a reality wishing for its birth
Blessing this brief second
That you exist on Mother Earth

And in one electric moment
With faith held high in hand
The space of God within you
Shall greet the great expand

Of consciousness reborn in love
The great belonging shall take place

An unimagined potential
Of oneness, love and grace

The waves of transformation
Reach out as pebbles entering pond
Dismantling humanity's self perception
Of collective emergence, a new dawn

~ Anita Pathik Law, June 18, 2012

Anita (Ani) Pathik Law, CFCC, CHt, *is a coach, hypnotherapist, lyricist, published author, speaker, healing facilitator, and a powerful voice in the consciousness movement. Author of The Power of Our Way; A Path to a Collective Consciousness, founder of The Power of Our Way Community and host of Conscious Dialogues, for over 17 years she has worked with thousands of people around the globe to help them "Raise Consciousness and Take Responsibility for Their Own Shift." Known as a "midwife to the soul," Anita has leveraged the power of the mind and spirit to overcome the seemingly impossible. She guides her clients to tap into their own mastery by awakening to and aligning with their soul's purpose to receive their inknown wisdom and gifts. A modern day shaman and energy alchemist who weaves both her East Indian heritage and indigenous spiritual practice into her work with healing and business clients, she offers a unique and spiritually grounded approach to all that she does and is in the world.*

Receive a powerful audio download of "A Declaration to Receive Your Good" at www.powerofmyway.com/ideclare.html

A HUGE Thank you to our Sponsors

Our commitment is to keep the cost of the Heal My Voice book circle projects low enough that all women have the opportunity to write and heal a story in their lives.

Thank you to the Sponsors who see the value of the work and who have supported the mission of Heal My Voice. We appreciate you.

Please check out their services and support them, too!

Awakening Essence. Awakening Humanity.™

www.essencecoaches.com

A HUGE Thank you to Essence Coaches for their support and honoring the work we are doing in the Heal My Voice projects.

To check out the services for a FEE and for FREE, Go To:

http://www.essencecoaches.com

THANK YOU!!

Check out the links to the websites of our sponsors. The projects would not be possible without them!

Nancy Mills
http://www.thespiritedwoman.com/

Adrienne MacDonald
www.cprsavinglives.com
www.thegiftoffocus.com

Adrienne Yeardye
www.alternativeoneness.com
www.jupitershive.com

Lisa Morningstar
http://leadbyintuition.com/

Deborah Stern
www.essencecoaches.com/deborahstern
www.2020strategies.net

Heal My Voice Projects

www.healmyvoice.org

Join us in our mission to help each woman discover her voice:

To Empower women and girls to heal grief, loss, and trauma, and reclaim their inner authority, so they can develop and use their leadership skills in their homes, communities, and the world, by developing collaborative, creative projects that encourage leadership, community building, and the reclaiming of each woman's voice.

"If we want our girls to benefit from the courage and wisdom of the women before them, we have to share the stories .-Shireen Dodson

Write your life so that others may be illuminated. ~**SARK**

"A woman's voice is the seat of her power and her compassion. A woman's word can heal or destroy; it can be a balm and a ballast, or it can be a source of divisiveness and destruction. A woman's voice is the seat of her power not only to choose her own destiny but also to manifest it. A woman's voice is a woman's choice." -**Yogi Bhajan...**

"The world will be saved by the western woman," said **the Dalai Lama** during the September 2009 Vancouver Peace Summit.

Healing Circle: Meditation and Energy Clearing-Tele-seminar Style:

Energy tools shared during a 30 minute meditation. FREE. Open to everyone. All of the Free links to the recordings of the monthly healing circle are available at **https://www.facebook.com/HealMyVoice** Click on Events and then Past Events.

Go to **www.healmyvoice.org** for the latest up to date news and projects.

Check out the Inward Journey Letter Circle, a woman's prison initiative: A collaboration with Heal My Voice and Imagine the Good Foundation.

Fearless Voices: True Stories by Courageous Women Facebook

Join us for more conversation:

https://www.facebook.com/FearlessVoices

Empowered Voices: True Stories by Awakened Women on Facebook

https://www.facebook.com/EmpoweredVoices

TO ORDER additional copies of this book and to discover additional Heal My Voice books in this series, go to the Heal My Voice website:

www.HealMyVoice.org

The Inward Journey Letter Circle (IJLC) is a program that connects women residing in the free world and women residing in prisons through a one-on-one letter-writing program. Through this connection we demonstrate that even across prison walls, there is a common bond and shared wisdom being activated now for the greater good.

IJLC is a program for women who are on a life journey of discovery both inward and outward. It is a program for women who recognize, honor, and embrace the shared wisdom that resides within us all. We are women who can imagine that we are not alone on this journey and that contributing to the greater good will change our world.

The IJLC brings women who reside in the free world and women who reside in the prisons into one circle. As women share their personal experiences along life's journey with their partners, together collectively and collaboratively they change the quality of their lives, the circle of partners, and the world.

If the Inward Journey Letter Circle speaks to you, if you feel the call to be a part of change for the good, then welcome! A journey to an unknown destination awaits you!

Contact Andrea Hylen, founder of Heal My Voice and Project Director for the Inward Journey Letter Circle. Email www.**healmyvoiceinc@gmail.com** for an application and orientation recording. There is a secret Facebook group and a monthly phone call to support women in the free world who are participating in the program.

(On the next page, words from a letter writer residing in prison and a poem.)

A Letter from Anitra: a woman in a prison in Arkansas. Written to her letter partner in the free world.

Letter One:

THANK YOU! for the beautiful letter. I have not cried often in here but I found myself balling like a baby throughout reading it. I could feel the energy coming off your letter. It has a true sense of compassion, understanding, support, encouragement + love. All the things I believe every human being craves and deserves. Something I believe I've lacked all my life. I found that the whole time I was reading it, the walls I've so carefully constructed around my heart had dissipated, leaving me feeling more free than I'd ever been.
I feel very connected to you already. Does that seem strange? I believe people cross paths for a reason + possibly this is a divine connection.

Letter Three:

My story has been at a standstill for a bit. The creative energy seems to be blocked right now. So I will wait for it to flow again + pick it up again then. I got to around page 90 before I stopped.
There are some things I've written about myself that I'd like to send you to read. Would you mind?
I hope you know that I appreciate the time you take to

write me. So many people tend to judge because of where I am. Others never bother to hear our stories. They fail to see that we once had dreams + goals, we just got lost along the way. Yet you have reached in a hand and given hope to this lost soul. I have hope in Jesus already, but with people like you it gives me hope in mankind.

Letter Four:

I want you to know that you inspire me + I appreciate the time you take for me. You are a blessing in my life.